The
Christmas Letters II

by Mark Mendizza

Larissa Press
Laguna Niguel, California

Larissa Press
Laguna Niguel, California

ISBN 978-1-7375107-2-7

First Edition

The Library of Congress Cataloging-in-Publication Data is available upon request.

Book design & graphics: Brian Ziegler

Published in the United States of America

To Grandpa Roy,
Wherever you are

A Christmas Letter is like kissing a joy as it flies by, and then singing about it.

— Mark Mendizza

Contents

Preface

Preface

This is not going to be pretty. It's going to be deep & jolly. It's going to be poignant. And it's going to be a "hoot" for sure, just like the first book – *The Christmas Letters, A Family. A Decade. A Hoot*. But it's not going to be pretty because the earlier book was about our goofy family in the nineties – a charmed decade – and this one is about the new Millennium, which began with . . . 9/11.

The charmed Nineties led off with the birth of our daughter Lara, the fall of Communism, and a bull market that ran for ten years straight. Without even knowing it, we made enough money for a Volvo and surfing lessons. It ended with a transcendent young girl twirling her way magically into the new Millennium. The letters not only lifted reader spirits, it also taught them how to use the Mayan calendar to outperform the Dow.

The next decade – this one – on the other hand, began with Al Qaeda. And then, another surprise attack: Lara became a teen. It ended with sub-prime lending, the collapse of the U.S. economy and Bernie Madoff. So, you can imagine.

That is why this book and its magically vacuous content is so important. It continues the work of sharing our crazy family with yours. As you read about our whacky moments you will recall all the whacky moments of your own and it will change the way you feel about things, especially Winter Formals and the U.S. Treasury Department. There are lots of adventures in the book, and lots of travel: Austria, Spain, Boston, Naples (Fl), Hawaii, The Eastern Sierra and The People's Republic of China. Through the sheer power of endearing anecdotes about learning how to drive, how to choose a dress for the Winter Formal, the thrill of victory, the agony of the college SAT, and a cast of famous people like Bill Murray, Andy Garcia and the irrepressible

Sylvester Stallone, you will forget about the decade of sub-prime lending and begin to view your past and present in a wholly different way; or your money back.

Seriously though. Since publishing the first book of Christmas Letters, readers have come to appreciate anew the ancient tradition of the form, which goes back 25,000 years to the cave paintings of Lascaux. Most uninformed people believe those paintings were Christmas Letters. As were the ancient Egyptian hieroglyphics — more talk about another royal family. And those signals from outer space? Right! Christmas Letters from a place far, far way. The point is, the tradition of telling stories about the family has been going on for Millennium. They contain truths and yes, "secrets" that are universal. And through this book, you will discover them all. Or maybe not.

What you will learn for sure; however, is that no matter the historical circumstance, EVERY decade, every year, every moment is full of wonder. That's what the book is all about: Our wonder, reaching out to yours.

"For everything that lives is Holy."

William Blake

2001

A Year of Infamy

2002

The Year of Two Trees

Mark, Sue & Lara Mendizza
Orange County, California

December 20, 2002

Dear Friends,

A spasm of panic percolated up from my lower abdomen, into my chest and throat, around the back of my neck, up over the bald spot (which is no longer a spot really; more like a "region") to my rutted brow, and I think even down into my teeth and cartilage, as Sue uttered the ominous words, "In five more days, Christmas will be over."

Over? I was thinking it was still early November. The Christmas trees should have tipped me off, but sometimes I miss things that are right in front of my eyes. Sue and Lara had spent the evening decorating the trees. I use the plural because two trees have become a minor Christmas tradition for us. (As you know, in the modern world anything that occurs twice in a row is considered a tradition, right up there with eggnog and shameless Christmas sweaters.). Sue decorates one tree and Lara decorates the other one. They don't compete. They put on a Christmas CD with music that was produced at Lara's school and they just do their own tree in their own unique and individual way. Lara tops her tree with a delightful glass snowman, and Sue tops hers with the handmade angel we obtained many years ago. I grumble through the entire tree decorating tradition. I complain about the scratches the trees caused on the roof of the car and the damage that will be done if we aren't very careful about the water we pour into the green bucket at the base of the tree. Whining is actually a Christmas tradition for me. But when they are done, I am always amazed at how beautiful the two trees are. This year, after they finished and turned on the lights, I thought they were especially stunning. They seemed like art, in their proportions, their glow, their quiet, compelling presence in the room. And I thought, the two trees in their unique beauty symbolized perfectly the wondrous beauty, intelligence and presence of their creators: Sue and Lara. And then I thought, boy am I lucky! In a heartbeat I went from "Christmas sucks" to "We should have these trees all year round."

I, of course, don't decorate. While Sue and Lara were out getting their trees, I was in the kitchen preparing a new soup from Andrew Weil's *I'm Way, Way Healthier Than You Are* Cookbook. When Sue and Lara drove up with the two Christmas trees tied to the roof like holiday road kill, I put on my pants. (Weil recommends cooking in one's underwear so the oxygen can travel more freely to the beard, which is where he and a lot of other bald people believe the soul resides.) I helped the girls untie the trees, carry them into the house, and position them, one in front of the living room window, so people who drive by our house can see what good people we are, and one in the family room for us to look at while we're watching the latest update on CNN's "Road to War in Iraq." As I was taking off my pants before going back to my soup, Sue uttered the words that cause vasoconstrictions all across the nation: "Only five more days til Christmas."

Not only haven't I given gifts a thought, I haven't thought about the annual Christmas letter either. We skipped the epistle last year because we were so stunned by the attacks on the nation. As important as our family is to us, our primary lenders and the kids in the neighborhood whose parents make them sell gift wrap to pay for their Christmas presents, we felt it would have been in poor taste to dwell on the new Suzanne Sommer's Thigh Enhancer that has had such a big impact on Sue's life. Judging from recent SUV sales, however, and the abundance of shows like "The World's Greatest Makeovers," we feel the nation has bounced back admirably and that maybe it would do our friends and colleagues some good to resume our yuletide tradition of inane, superficial self-absorption: namely, The Christmas Letter.

The only question is time. I have two hours before I have to meet a client about a national ad campaign for a new style of nail. So OK: two hours, two years. Here goes:

First let's cover the news from Southern California. When we left off at the end of the year 2000, the Supreme Court had just anointed George Bush president of the United States, and the state of California had mysteriously run out of energy. (And I'm not saying these two events were in any way related.) We were accused of being a fuzzy-logic, moonbeam state that could not plan properly for energy needs (a euphemistic way oil company executives have of saying we should have built more power

15

plants). In order to keep the lights on, our leaders were forced to enter into usurious contracts with Texas energy brokers. Today, of course, we know those Texas guys, right after meeting with Vice President Dick Cheney about the nation's energy policy, pulled a high-energy "longhorn" fast one on all of us. (And I'm not saying these two events were in any way related.) Today, the state of emergency is over, the lights are on (especially across the street where the reindeers on Sarah's house have been designated by NASA as an official earth coordinate for astronauts returning to earth) and our moonbeam state is $34 billion in the red.

I know. I know. What does $34 billion have to do with the Mendizza family? And that's just it: a lot. This morning, for example, I got up and as I do every morning, gave Sue a big, affectionate hug and asked her what she had planned for the day. (You guys may want to try this. A few simple hugs and you get to choose the sitcom you watch with your mate while you're waiting for the kids to fall asleep, so you can you-know-what.) Sue's response was telling. "I have to get these cookies to the jail, today," she said, sweetly as always, but pensive. I immediately made the connection. Cookies for the jail! The $34B deficit has forced Sue to pay for the cookies she delivers to the inmates within the Orange County Jail system. Let me be clear: She does not have to buy cookies, and sometimes she even withholds the chocolate covered macaroons from the really nasty white nationalists, but when the Christmas spirit overcomes her, which happens every year about this time, Sue cannot resist it. She borrows someone's Costco card and a pick-up truck, and she buys cookies for the inmates.

As you may recall, Sue took a sabbatical two years ago and

she so enjoyed the leisurely pace and reduced stress level that when it was time to report back to work she asked to be placed back in the classroom instead assuming the administrative responsibilities she had been handling before her sabbatical; namely, coordinating the College's educational programs inside the County Jail system and listening to me explain about the Higgs boson. But after a year of teaching, the peace and tranquility became more than she could stand and asked to be sent back into the "fray." Today, Sue is the coordinator of the Santiago College Inmate Education program and as the leader she feels the need to get everyone cookies, including teachers, staff and all the minor drug offenders, who make up about 90% of the inmates. Is there a link between Sue's vanished cookie budget, Enron, the state deficits, and the meeting all those Texas oil guys had with the Vice President? I'm not saying that. I'm just saying there may be some dots here, and when you connect the dots, you may not get a picture of Frosty the Snowman.

Locally, of course, the big news this year was the Anaheim Angels. They won the World Series, and in doing so restored the faith that Southern Californians had in miracles and the ability of common men to transform water into wine, or gold, or in this case hard currency. Not water exactly, but warm, flat beer that tastes like something out of Lake Erie. I mean have you ever had a beer at Anaheim Stadium; or, sorry: I mean Edison Field? Even when the Angels were losing, like before they started using steel bats, the beer was over $6.50 a cup. Not since Moses has man performed such a feat: a soggy cup of flat, stale, watery whatever, transformed before our very eyes into $7.50. It's almost as bad as the movie theaters where people have been forced to actually pay for their popcorn and Pepsi on the installment plan.

The baseball was good, of course; and during the entire post-season play the Angels were so relentless they made Rocky and the Terminator seem like quitters, especially that little guy Eckstein. He's the only guy ever to make it to the big leagues without having a strike zone. You probably recall the way Troy Percival had to squint hard before every pitch he threw. That's because of Eckstein. Percival has been pitching to Eckstein during Angel practices for several years, and he says he's never yet actually seen the guy. "Some pitchers have gone blind, looking for Eckstein at the plate," says Percival, who had 20/20 vision before he was traded to Anaheim. "I've been lucky."

The impact of the 2002 Angel saga on our family was profound. First of all, Sue was actually overheard saying, "Maybe I should give up on Cleveland and become an Angel fan." Sue was born and raised in Cleveland, and back when the Indians were contenders for the pennant, she had to be sedated, lest she harm herself or others with her outbursts. This year, however, Sue was glued to the set; I mean she gave up a spa facial once to watch the pre-game show. The Angel team was so seductive, though, that even I started watching the games and listening to them on the radio, as I schlepped Lara back and forth to auditions and rehearsals and her theater performances. (More about that later, of course.) I stopped being interested in professional sports the day free-agency became a fixed part of the game. I liked the old days when the players were poor, when the adulation and sex they received from fans was sufficient compensation for whatever hitting, catching and throwing of the ball they did; which, aside from spitting on their shoes and adjusting testicles on T.V., is what baseball players are all about. The 2002 Angel team, however, was different. The "Halos" were Shakespearean in theme, operatic in grandeur and refreshingly hygienic in terms of where team members placed their hands when the camera was on them.

Which brings me to Lara's new school and her work at the Laguna Beach Playhouse, an equally "dramatic" sequence of events.

Bragging Begins Here

This is the point in the Christmas Letter where bragging about one's kid is concealed behind a façade of factual reporting. When I say, for example, that Lara auditioned and was accepted at a cool performing arts high school like the one in the movie, FAME, what I am really saying is that I have reached that stage in the parenting process where one finally gives up on one's own pathetic, meaningless life and begins to live vicariously in the achievements of one's offspring. In short, Lara's achievements have become my achievements. This premise expanded so far inside my mind that after Lara received her acceptance letter, I thought it was actually me who was accepted at the Orange County High School of the Performing Arts. I bought tights, tap shoes and those calve-warmers, plus one of those canvas bags you see performers throw over their shoulders on their way to rehearsal, and I reported bright and early to class. After several weeks of counseling I gradually realized that it was Lara and not me who they wanted in their school. So, I'm back to dividing my time between schlepping my daughter around town and working – part time – with my team on high-energy particle physics.

The last time we wrote to you Lara was still in sixth grade I think, doing the usual reports on the Mayan and Aztec Indians, which kids in this school district must do every year until they graduate. Now she's in eighth. She successfully made the transition to middle school, where she was probably the smallest of the 2,000 kids enrolled (Her friends actually took turns carrying Lara from class to class inside their backpacks.) Then we heard about this performing arts school (OCHSA) where instead of trying to decide whether to go "gothic" or to the mall, the kids danced and sang in the hallways between classes, just like in FAME. That sounded good, and so we made inquiries. "You fill out an application and make an appointment for an audition," they said. And it seems like we've been auditioning ever since. (See: I said "we" again. The therapists were right when they told me, you're never cured of vicarious living, especially the parental kind. You just have to learn to live with it.) For kids seeking entrance to eighth grade, the applications were due a few months into the first semester of seventh. So, we figured we could apply and then decide later about whether Lara should actually change schools (There were lots of consequences to such a choice: leaving very good friends, compromising her pathway to MIT, which we had charted on our wall next to the Periodic Table of the Elements, and of course giving up the Mayans and Aztecs.) We worked hard to falsify resumes and applications for several art areas, including Creative Writing, Musical Theater, Commercial Dance, Film & Television and Celebrity Prep I, which was a new specialty. Sue took the stack of apps to the school and stood in line with hundreds of other parents. When she reached the front and handed the paperwork over to the woman behind the table, the woman looked through them and then looked up at Sue and said, "Would your daughter like to audition for this year?" Whoa! They had an opening in the

Film and Television department for seventh grade. Should "we" try for it? Are "we" prepared? Lara has made two small movies which we had included in the applications; one called Killing Mr. Bonce, a murder mystery she made in two hours with her friends during her 11th birthday party, and one called, How to Make a Movie, which was a cute documentary about (OK. Let's see if you can guess what it was about). Several days later we received a call from the head of the department to set up an interview/audition.

I swear, I could write a whole Christmas Letter about this auditioning process. Over time, Lara has grown accustomed to it, but when it's new, it can be so very scary and intimidating, especially for parents living vicariously. Walking into a strange room, in front a group of strange people and presenting oneself with the goal of convincing them that one has the gifts and skills and talents worthy of … whatever the hell the strangers want. But if one can sort of get used to it, and get good at it, then that itself becomes an important life skill, at least in my view. And Lara has acquired a genuine internal strength I think, through her work over the last year and a half.

Sue, Lara and I drove together to the school for the audition with the director of the Film and Television department. I cannot tell you how nervous we were, and how hard we tried to pretend that we weren't, that everything was cool. We got it handled. We're good. Think positive. No negs. Only pluses. We can't lose, here. Life is so much bigger than this dumb ol' audition. We don't really care that much, anyway. Let's turn around, OK?

On the way I gave Lara some tips: "Visualize, honey. Are you visualizing? And breathe. Are you breathing? Sometimes I listen to Metallica to pump me up before an important meeting.

Do you want to listen to Metallica, sweetheart?" I put on a tune called, Scurvy, Warts and Enemas are What I Love. As it broke out the back window of the car, I yelled to Lara in the back seat, "How do you feel, sweetie? Is this good for you? Do you feel pumped up?"

We arrived at the school. Sue and I escorted Lara to the office where the department head was waiting to grill our daughter. Who the hell is this guy, anyway? What does he know about Lara, how wonderful she is, how sensitive, intelligent and kind? Darn it! I think I better do this audition myself. Sue takes my arm and escorts me back to the car. We drive away, leaving Lara to do the audition on her own, to confront the director and "world" on her own.

We went back about an hour and a half later. We walked back into the building where the office was located and looked for Lara. We found her and the director in an editing room, talking together. "Hi," I said, cheerfully, as if we'd just got back from the spa. "Hi," Lara responded. It looked like they were finished with their formal interview, but there was no way to tell how it went. For a while we made small talk there in the editing room. The director was very kind, very respectful of Lara and her work. He complimented her on her movies, on the discussions he and she had had. It all felt very good, but what was the ultimate outcome? Is he going to tell us? Is she in or out? Finally, after dragging the pleasantries out for as long as I could, I simply blurted out, "Will you accept her to the department?" He paused and said, "We would love to have Lara join us."

Oh my god. How can our emotional lives become so damn dependent on so few words? I mean we kept it cool, just back from the spa, totally relaxed, looks like it might rain. But inside

I'm going "oh goodie, goodie, goodie. Life is so good. Lara did it. She encountered the director and the 'world' and she won."

That was her first sort of big audition. Since then it seems like she is auditioning every twenty minutes. It is still a tense and apprehensive thing, but with the help of some incredibly talented and more important, incredibly compassionate people, Lara has gradually built an inner strength that helps. She has learned to prepare; to present; walk in, give it her best shot, and then move on. It's been a gift; from The OCHSA experience, but even more from the work she has done at the Laguna Beach Playhouse.

She had to audition to get into their program as well. I think she had to sing and perform a monologue. There are hundreds of books that contain monologues for just this purpose, for actors to use when they are auditioning to get a role in a play, or into a school, or to get a date, or impress people at parties, or get out of a DUI situation, or past security, or to just amuse oneself in front of the mirror. The point is, one needs to memorize a few good monologues and have them at one's disposal for whatever need might arise, and there are hundreds of little books full of monologues created by actors who were never cast. Lara and I scanned dozens of these books, but they all seemed rather flat. So we worked together to write our own. Here's one she used to audition for a play called *Anastasia Krupnik*, which is a touching little comedy about a ten year old Jewish girl, her family and ten year old Irish Catholic friend.

God's Plan

I believe we're here for a purpose. I mean God placed us here on earth for a reason, right? Otherwise, nothing would make much sense. Like,

23

why go to school for sixteen years, when we could be, like: at the mall. (And that doesn't include graduate school. Can you believe I'm twelve, and my parents have already signed me up for grad school.)? Part of God's plan, they say.

Or why study the Aztec Indians in fourth, fifth, sixth AND seventh grade? I mean, did they run out of history? Do you know how many times I had to draw pictures of Quetzocotl and the Conquistadors, just so our teachers have something to put on the wall during Open House? Part of the plan. Has to be. Otherwise it 's like, ridiculous.

Same with vegetables. Why would anybody eat a bowl of Brussel Sprouts or BEETS, if it weren't part of a bigger plan. That's what faith is. The absolute total belief in something we know absolutely nothing about.

For example: I was placed here to teach my parents a lesson: In patience. I'm sort of a test. If they pass, they get to go to heaven where there are no kids. If they don't, they have to be parents again, til they get it right.

I have lots of ways to test my parents. One I call the "OK-I know" technique. This one drives them crazy. They ask me to do something, like turn off the television, or do my homework or eat – BEETS. I always respond with a cheerful, "OK. I know."

My parents walk away, thinking they have accomplished something. But of course, they haven't. I don't turn off the T.V., do my homework or eat the beets. My parents come back in like a half an hour, and they're like all, WHAT?! You haven't done what we said? That just cracks me up. And then they say the same thing, only a lot louder. "Turn off the T.V. Do your homework. Eat your beets."

OK. Like there's no way I'm going to eat those beets. If God himself came down and asked me to eat the beets, I'd like . . . well, I'd negotiate. But with my parents, I'm totally poised, totally in tune with God's plan for me. I respond with a cordial, "OK. I know."

I can't believe it's that easy, but that's all it seems to take to get them to go away, again. But they like always come back and see I haven't done anything, and raise the volume even louder. We do this three or four times until my Dad's face is the color of those beets. He screams. I move. My Dad gets a "D" on the test. He'll probably have to repeat parenting.

But it teaches him patience. Which is my purpose. The reason I was placed here on earth. I love my parents a lot. And sometimes it's not easy for me to be so tough on them. But it's because I love them that I do it. I'd do anything for them. Except the beet thing. Beets were a mistake. I mean everyone makes mistakes, right. Even . . . well: everybody.

Tons of kids auditioned for the play. The first round is like a cattle call where everyone shows up and gives a reading. Then they have "call backs." Call backs are awful because you wait and wait so pensively to hear if you get one. To get a call back is like winning a bronze medal. The phone rings. You pick it up. It's them. It's the theater. Oh my god! "Could Lara come back on Monday night at 6:00?" Oh, yea, sure. Sure. Nice weather, huh? You try to stay calm.

So Lara went back, and instead of reading the monologue,

she and the other "call backs" read a piece directly from the play. Then you go home again, and wait. Go to school. Play with friends. Do homework. And wait for guess what? Right. Another call-back. And Lara got one. Yes! It's like getting a silver.

The list of actors has now been reduced to just a few. They all go back and the director has them read with different people. The director usually has a vision of what he or she (In this case it was Donna) would like the play to become, and fulfilling that vision depends on many, many factors; but casting is key. (I think it was Robert Altman who said after he has finished casting a film, it's about 90% done.) By this time Lara knows that all the actors are great, that they all come close to fulfilling Donna's vision, and that it's down to small details. It could be something as incidental as body type, or voice tone, or a gesture the director is looking for and that she doesn't know she's even looking for it until she sees it. And so, Lara just gives it her best shot.

At the end of the session, Donna brought in the three girls who were contending for the role of Jennifer, Anastasia's Irish Catholic friend. First, she said to them all, "Thank you so much for coming here and working so hard. You are all just splendid actors." Then she turned to Kim and said, "Kim." Donna always addresses the kids directly, with a profound caring and respect and love that distinguishes the program at Laguna Beach from any other children's theater I have ever seen. She said, "Kim, thank you for your hard work. All three of you we're so good that this was a very difficult decision." Lara was standing there with Kim and Janice. Inside, she was pretty sure that Janice was going to get the part. No matter how much you may visualize; no matter how much Metallica you listen to, you always feel a little inadequate. But then something extraordinary happened. Donna turned to Janice and said, "Janice, thank you so much for coming in so many times. It was a hard decision because you are all so talented." At that moment, of course, Lara knew. She knew. But she didn't move. She stood there and looked at Donna. And Donna turned to her and said, "Lara, would you be our Jennifer?"

When I heard how Donna had handled this process, I just wanted to get down on my hands and knees and thank God for her and Joe and Kelly and Diane; everyone who has helped create such an astonishing level of excellence. It is fiercely competitive and thus replete with the hope and disappointment and envy and all the other difficulties that human flesh is heir to, and yet maintained a level of compassion and love and almost selfless support between the adults and kids, equity actors and kids, and perhaps most important the parents and theater and kids. To me, it was profound, and I did get down on my knees until a crowd started to gathering and some guy used his cell phone to call 911, and Lara said I was embarrassing her.

Jennifer was a principle role in a fabulous production with a world-class group of principle actors, and Lara just nailed the role. At one point in the show Anastasia is sort of impatient and at the same time concerned about the fact that her mother is having a baby. She says to Jennifer, "My mother is having a baby." And Lara (Jennifer), who is Irish Catholic and so very used to babies, says, "Oh, my mother has them all the time." And the audience just cracked up. And Sue breathed again. And I promised God I would tithe, starting Monday.

After Anastasia, Lara was cast as a munchkin in *The Wizard of Oz*. Earlier she played a flamingo in *Alice in Wonderland*. And last Tuesday we watched her crawl across the stage with an enormous shell on her back in a little piece about the *Tortoise and the Hare*. There is one thing about this theater business that I think distinguishes it from other youth activities like organized sports, and that is the fact that one day a child might be center stage, in the spotlight, a star; and then a week later the same child will be cleaning between the seats of the theater, taking tickets or moving sets backstage. In sports, the star is usually the star all day long. "We" feel so blessed.

Franz Shubert

OK. I have to hurry, now. I only have twenty minutes.

Did I tell you about the $5,000 dachshund we got? It's true. We bought a little puppy – Penny — which of course we fell in love with. (We named her Penny because of the color of her beautiful coat, not how much we paid. If we would have named her according to price, we would have name her "Fortune." As you likely know from our previous book, *The Christmas Letters, A Family. A Decade. A Hoot!*, we began 1988 with Fergie, a miniature dachshund that brought more love and joy into our lives than a room full of saints. After Fergie rose up to heaven, we waited a year and then brought Penny home. It sounds nuts, but even after having Fergie for years, we still couldn't remember anything about how to potty train an puppy. I swear to god we thought if we just whacked it enough times with the paper, it would figure the whole thing out. We built barriers to contain little Penny inside the kitchen, but while we were out she immediately lay siege, and when we returned the walls had been breached and revenge had been taken on the white carpet. In fact, the carpet became her private potty for six months, and by the time she learned to use the toilet, it was pretty much an out-house. Ka Ching! $5,000 dachshund. Now she sits on the com-mode and takes a leisurely "Schubert" while reading the funnies, just like the rest of us.

"Schubert?" You don't know what a "Schubert" is because you weren't there when we invented it. Here's the Shubert story. In the car. Riding with four thirteen-year-old girls on the way to school. Lara's new school is in downtown Santa Ana and so the BPSTC (Beleaguered Parents Society of Trabuco Canyon) or-ganized a carpool with the other kids in our area who make the commute. I take my turn, and actually enjoy it. It's a little window into the life Lara has outside of the nest, so to speak.

The five of us usually wake up when we cross the border into Irvine. From there to Santa Ana we pretty much party. As we enter a tunnel the girls suddenly hold their breath until we exit. If you don't, something bad will happen. You'll be assigned a seat next to a boy with a reputation for adult-like flatulence, or you'll get a teacher who pretends to be young. When I drive over rail-road tracks, the girls raise their feet up off the floor until we've crossed them. This saves lives. Each time we cross the tracks and Lara, Katie, Chelsea and Alex raise their feet, their magic is such that a train wreck somewhere in the world is averted, a thief on the verge of taking something that does not belong to him has a second thought, a terrorist slips in the shower, hits his head and changes his mind. (Alhamduallah)

The girls talk and joke and tease just like boys, except they're not quite as vulgar. And of course we fight over the radio. Alex has all the station call numbers memorized and calls them out, 101.2, 93.5, 89.4. To me, the songs sound like they were all writ-ten by the same girl, the blond with the pants made of neon-colored shrink-wrap. We listen to "He was a boy. She was a girl" for a few minutes and then I make my parental declaration: "Time for Schubert." I turn to the classical music channel, and no matter what piece is playing, I say, "Schubert's Second in C or Schubert's Cello Concerto." I've told the girls that this station only plays stuff by Schubert, and since no one in the car knows the difference between Schubert, Schumann or Schostakovich, there is a skeptical but almost tacit acceptance. And then a unanimous groan. I've been switching to Schubert all year, with the same response, and the name has become associated with a certain kind of mature, unpleasant dullness of tone.

Surprisingly, it was Lara who discovered a new association. "Schubert sounds like . . ." and she uttered the "Sh" sound from the "Sh" word that she has probably never uttered but has certainly heard Daddy recite at appropriate moments, like when he discovers the milk carton has been put back into the refrigerator WITH NO MILK, or the e-mail provider is down, or the bathroom scale gives yet another impossible reading, or you know, like the sun comes up at the wrong time. Katie and Alex pick up on it. "Ah, Schubert!" says Katie, the way I might say it when a traffic light I thought I would get through turns red. Everyone laughs. "Yea," says Alex. "Like she kicked the "Schubert" out of him." Chelsea, with her background in classical music, thinks this may be a sacrilege, but then gives it up and says, "He's in the bathroom, taking a 'Schubert.'" I mean we're into frat house mode, now. I'm laughing so hard I drive past the school. Lara screams, "If you don't turn around, Dad, we're all going to be in some deep 'Schubert.'"

And the socks. Remember back in 1996 or 1997 when I told you about how we spent the second half of the year looking for socks that disappeared, mostly Lara's. You do the wash and when you take the socks out and try to pair them up you only have one of each, never two. We actually called in a private investigator to try and get to the bottom of the mystery. And then two days ago, Sue figured it out. "Look!" she yelled as she was folding a basket of clothes. She held up two socks that looked quite different. Then she turned one of the socks inside out and held it up to the other one and Ouila! They matched. Sue has decided to quit her job at the jail and write a book about it.

And we celebrated our 15th wedding anniversary this year. This was special, and boy is Sue lucky to have a husband like me! Listen to this. I created a handmade anniversary card and sent it to her at work. I think it arrived on her desk about September 25th. And you can imagine how touched Sue was when she opened it. She called me immediately and expressed her gratitude and affection and then, in an ever so gentle shift in tone that only Sue is able to pull of with complete sincerity, she said "But sweetheart. Our anniversary is in November."

Lara had surgery this year, too. Back in January I think. For her entire life this little girl has had enlarged and usually infected tubernates, which are cartilage structures inside the nasal cavity that are used to make your nose too big. As a result, Lara has had chronic breathing problems her entire life, and we finally decided that in addition to good a strict military discipline and limits on television viewing, a growing child also needs air. So, the doctor surgically reduced the size of her tubernates. After she came out of the OR, however, Sue and I were crushed. What have we done? To see her unconscious, and so battered and swollen was very painful. The bandages on her face looked like a cast, and lucky for us her friend Deena walked into the room, took one look at Lara and said, "Hey, can I sign your nose?"

Lara and I have been going to the ballet together for the last several years as a kind of father-daughter thing, though I'm not sure why other stuff like nagging isn't considered a father-daughter thing, too. We've seen a lot of the world's finest ballet companies and frankly we were getting a little tired of swans and tutus, so we tried a modern dance company this year. It was called the Mark Morris Dance Company. And how wonderful was that? The thing that distinguished this company from others is that it travels with its own music ensemble and vocalist, so it wasn't forced to use recorded tracks. And instead of a fair maiden being dragged off the stage by an evil prince with thighs like Greek Doric columns, there were normal characters like you and me, only they could dance (which actually makes them way different than me). The creative combination of song, music, dance and story was just superb. And I remember as the vocalist sang this exquisite version of "Someone to Watch Over Me." I leaned over to Lara during the dance number that took place at a soda fountain instead of an enchanted forest and said, "I'm liking this." She said, "Shhhh!"

In the car, on the way to the theater, we reviewed the electromagnetic spectrum. Lara had a test on it the next day, and the only way Sue would let us go to the ballet was if we studied on the way. We talked about the absorption and the reflection of light and how that, plus something called pigment, created colors. We talked about mechanical waves and electromagnetic waves. "Electromagnetic waves can exist in a vacuum," I explained. "Mechanical waves must have a medium, like air or water. The light from stars, for example, is electromagnetic." I opened the sunroof of the car, and said, "Look. find a star."

"The light from that star, the light that is landing on the retina of your eye this very moment has traveled probably ten million years, at the speed of about 186,000 miles per second, through a vacuum, which is why it only took ten million years. Sound waves, seismic waves, and the waves of the ocean have to have a medium to go through. Electromagnetic waves don't. They can travel through empty space." We talked about wavelengths and their properties. And eventually got to the color magenta, which is one of the secondary colors.

Later, while walking through the lobby of the theater, Lara caught sight of a middle-aged woman in the crowd. "She had like this hair that was sort of brown or gray or something," she said, "and then right up here by her forehead she had this bright spot of magenta. It was weird. I mean hair with a secondary color." When we got to our seats in the balcony, Lara leaned over the edge and actually found the woman in the seats below. "There she is," she said, "the woman with the magenta hair." I leaned over, too. Down below I saw a young couple kissing in their seats. I put my hand over Lara's eyes. I leaned over a little more and found her, the middle-aged woman with the magenta hair. I settled back into my seat. Lara turned to me. "She's kind of old," she said. "She's trying to stay young," I responded. "Nothing wrong with that." And then I told her about my idea to dye my own hair a cool shade of cyan.

The Donner Party

In April, Lara and I took a rock climbing and backpacking trip into the wilderness at Joshua Tree National Park. We signed up for the trip with an organization called Donner Party Excursions. It was one of those trips where one has to be absolutely self-sufficient, no franchise food places, no versatellers, no Starbucks. To prepare, Lara and I attended seminars on how to survive in the Mojave with nothing to eat but other campers. We learned what to wear (layers of polyester attire that can be purchased only from the Donner Party Survival Boutique), how to pack the backpack (stuff everything down to the bottom, except the Game Boy and Survival Fudge Bars), how to scale sheer one hundred foot rock faces with just some rope, a mechanical device called a carabiner, and a really strong person that you are absolutely certain likes you a lot, to hold on to the rope.

It was a very cool trip. Lara and I rock climbed all day on Friday. Even though you have a rope and carabiners and a strong guy who likes you, it's still scary and in my opinion verges on the super-human. Lara climbed the damn thing like Spiderwoman. I was more like Elephant Man. The key is overcoming the paralyzing fear and then making a move on the cliff face when there is simply no conceivable move to make. You're stuck on the rock, eighty-five feet above the ground. Your face is smashed into the side of the cliff. You're hanging onto a crevice just big enough to insert maybe two fingers to the second knuckle, and you're struggling to maintain a foothold on a chink in the rock the thickness of your Mont Blanc pen. There's nothing to reach up to above you and no other footholds below you. You look down and you plead with tears in your eyes to the guide from Donner Party Excursions, "What do I do?" He looks up and says, "Go up!" It takes unusual balance, strength and a certain kind of mental deficiency, but it's exhilarating when you get to the top, and you can use the word carabiner at parties.

We camped that night, and in the morning, with packs on

our backs that weighed as much as Volkswagens, we headed out into the wilderness. Lara was awesome. She is small, and carrying twice her body weight, plus some of mine, on her back. There was only a little whining, all of which was coming from me. At night the group laid out under the stars and different members told stories about the adventures they'd had. The guide from the Donner Party told us all about how he climbed Mount Kilamanjaro in Kenya. Lara told about climbing the pyramids at Chichen Itza, on the Yucatan Peninsula. I told about how one year I climbed up and strung the Christmas lights on our house without even hiring one of those college kids who charge $300, taking them down not included.

It was days of grueling forced hikes and physical challenges known only to the likes of Sherpas, survivalists and people forced by circumstance to work as personal assistants, but we made it back home safely. Lara had finally gotten out of her soiled clothes, taken a bath, played with her puppy, and, after walking back downstairs and doing a twirl in front of Mommy and I said, "Oh, I just love the great indoors."

Ole!

And then there was Spain! Oh my gosh. I only have ten minutes left, and I haven't told you about Spain. We went there in August. I had gone to a performance of Flamenco song and dance in Los Angeles about two years ago and after hearing the song and seeing the dance first hand, as opposed to T.V. versions, I was totally captivated by the art form. When Sue asked, where should we go for vacation, I said Spain. I said I want to become a Gypsy and sing like that.

The first thing one notices after clearing customs and entering the baggage area of the airport in Madrid is that Spain is aflame. It's on fire! And I'm not talking the Spanish passion for the bullfight and Flamenco. I'm talking Spanish smokers. I'm saying Spain has not received the memo about the smoke-free workplace. "They are all smoking," said Lara as we wheeled our baggage out from the billowing plumes of smoke inside the terminal to the taxi stand. "And they're all speaking Spanish, too," I replied with my deep insight into foreign culture.

Our goal was to spend a few nights in Madrid, see whatever Flamenco we could find in the capital (the "real stuff" occurs down south where the Gypsies live), check out the Goyas at the Prado, and see Picasso's Guernica, which had finally been returned to the country. After painting the enormous canvas about the merciless bombing of a Basque city by Germans during the Spanish Civil war, Picasso said it could not be placed anywhere on Spanish soil until the last vestiges of fascism had been expelled. (Which occurred last Wednesday.) After seeing the capital, we planned to go south to Andalusia, the home of Gypsy culture and Flamenco. And we almost made it.

I wish I had time to discuss the entire history of the Spanish people from the pre-history of the Iberian Peninsula when tribal people first began fighting over copyrights for those stick figures they drew on the walls of their caves; to the Golden Age during which the Spanish Empire actually exceeded the square footage the Romans had achieved, and then forced native Americans in Florida and South America to name all their streets after a guy named Alfonso; to the fall from grace which witnessed the poor Spanish lose just about every war they started, beginning with the big Armada fiasco where they lost the entire fleet to a girl; to the sad Spanish Civil War and rise of fascism, which put the nation all the way back to GO; to the present time where they are becoming a world player again by inventing Rafael Nadal. But I don't have time for all that history. Let's just say Spain is unique. And relevant, especially to Spaniards.

We discovered a very cool place in Madrid called Casa Patas. It's a hang out for Gypsy families that make their living performing flamenco. The artists are authentic, the song deep, the dance explosive. We arrived at about 8:00 for dinner and had to wait for a few minutes while the proprietor finished laughing. "Maybe I said it wrong," I told Sue and Lara. So Sue tried. She is fluent in Spanish. She'll have better luck. This time all the waiters and even a few people from the street began to laugh. "8:00 for dinner?!" Once he caught his breath, the head guy told us that no one eats dinner in Madrid before 10:00, which of course is our bedtime.

The show began at midnight and went on til about 2:00. A couple of guys with guitars, a couple of vocalists, a female dancer. And one Roadie. No amps. No special effects. Just hypnotic handclapping and Cante Jondo. But for me, the spectacle surpassed in spirit and intensity almost anything going on in our electronic era of high wattage art. Not everyone feels that way, I know. Like Lara and Sue, for example. Lara fell asleep across Sue's lap at about one in the morning, and as I was thinking about giving up my citizenship and joining a Gypsy commune in Cadiz, Sue I think was wondering whether there was anything like a Gypsy Spa.

The next day, we actually got robbed on the streets of Madrid. The three of us were strolling down a very large boulevard on a balmy Spanish day, when we walked by a man begging on a corner. He was crouched against the side of a building, his head down, his hand up and outstretched. After a while, you get upset with yourself for turning down so many needy people when they approach you on the street for money. So, I just walked over and placed some Euros into the man's hand. We continued walking. A few minutes later, the same man came running up to us, sort of waving his hands and trying to say something to us, to warn us. I thought, oh great. Now he wants to come home and live with us. But that wasn't it. The guy was trying to alert us. Finally, Sue made out what he was saying. We'd been robbed. He had seen it. They took Sue's wallet right out of her backpack. Lara and I had been right behind her, and yet we didn't even notice. And guess who the culprits were? Ole! Gypsies. Five Gypsy women had walked by and made the move on us. But we didn't care that much. I mean after the night at Casa Patas I was practically a Gypsy myself. Besides, we had Gold Cards. And there was an office within blocks. We gave our new friend enough Euros to buy a small house. Then we went to the American Express office, where they issued new cards and sold us some Gypsy Insurance. It took a little longer than we thought it would, but soon we were on the bullet train down to Seville.

In Seville, we were just getting ready to make the next leg of our trip down toward Jerez and Cadiz and the other little villages known throughout the world as the place where "true" flamenco still flourishes, when we received a phone call from the states. Sue's mom had fallen and broken her hip. Ole! Trip over. And all my time is up.

The one great thing about the terrible tragedy of having to

give up our quest for true Flamenco was that Delta Airlines flew us back first class, and I think Lara liked that at least as much as she would have liked six more nights of fiery foot stomping. And she really didn't want her Daddy to join a Gypsy clan and live in a wagon.

Just a few notes before we close with our Christmas wish.

My friend Brian Ziegler, had a baby, or rather his wife, Denise, did. He's an artist, but his daughter, Kat, is his finest creation.

My brother got married to a beautiful woman named Zdenka from the Czech Republic. She's going to spend 2003 explaining about their use of consonants, which we're all looking forward to.

Do you remember Raphael? He left his work for human rights at Harvard and took a job at the United Nations. He's in Sierra Leone today, working to reconcile conflicts there, which is like reconciling all the conflicts in "As the World Turns."

You're all probably wondering about my book. OK. My agent is driving in her limousine from Manhattan out to her house in the Hamptons. She feels guilty because she hasn't sold my book and she doesn't know if she can sell it. So she picks up her cell phone and she calls me. She tells me how great I am and then says, "Mark." And I'm like, go ahead. I can handle it. If Lara can handle it, then I can handle it. She says, "Mark, I don't think you have cracked the code. You are a charming writer. I love your book. But I could not get publishers to pay my usual gazillion dollars for it, and I need to pay for the house in the Hamptons." No. She didn't say that. Suzanne is one of the best agents in the business, knowing, tough and caring; not to mention head of the literary department at William Morris. She just couldn't get publishers to move off the dime. She said write another one, and we'll sell them both. Write a novel, she said. So that's what we're, or rather, that's what I am doing. It's about a regular guy, a family man, a weekend cyclist who becomes the new Messiah.

Regarding particle physics and my work with MIT, here's the scoop on that: The mystery remains. This may be a little over your head and if it is, don't worry. There are only a few of us who really understand this stuff, and the other two guys are part time.

OK. So about three months ago Lara had finally put the finishing touches on her report about the Pygmy Marmoset, the smallest monkey in the world, and yes: genetically it appears to have a genome virtually identical to Rudy Giuliani. That night, Sue and I decided to celebrate the achievement by going to the movies. We went to the local multi-plex which offered several hundred choices, all of which claimed to be better than sitting home. On my recommendation, we tried *Sum of All Fears,* but walked out because it became immediately clear Ben Affleck was not smart enough to stop an impending nuclear war. We walked out of the second one, too because it didn't have a cartoon. Finally, Sue says, "We're going to see *My Big Fat Greek Wedding.* Of course, I resisted. I didn't think it possessed the gravitas necessary to celebrate the completion of the Marmoset treatise. But it turned out there were lots of illusive philosophical questions imbedded in the film that only a few of us were able to appreciate, like the fact that Greek families are just like everybody else's except they break plates and know how to say Agamemnon.

After the movie we had a taste for kabob. We went to

THE CHRISTMAS LETTERS II

the Persian restaurant we liked, but it was closed. Huh? Eight o'clock and its closed? Apparently Persians have their own time, in which they have to go to bed earlier than the Spanish. So, we drove to the Thai place and had some coconut soup and Larb Gai. That's where I "man-splained" the problem we were having with the universe.

I told Sue how I'd been thinking about John Wheeler, one of America's foremost theoretical physicists. "He worked with Bohr," I said. Sue asked for chop sticks. "Worked with Einstein, too. Worked with Feynman. Wheeler was the one who corrected the math in quantum physics, and I read recently where he had speculated that reality does not exist until it is observed." "May I have the condiment tray?" asked Sue.

Actually, she did remember a play I made us go see called *Copenhagen*, and she pointed out that Neils Bohr had said something similar, something about uncertainty.

"Right," I said, pretty excited. "Heisenberg and Bohr had worked out the uncertainty principle. It's been verified. It's a law of indeterminacy. One cannot know both the velocity of a particle and its position at the same time. Period. So "uncertainty" is part of every calculation involving the movement and position of particles in the quantum world – and that's basically all anyone does in the quantum world is measure movement and position of particles, and maybe an occasional collision. So, when you're looking at anything smaller than a billionth of a billionth of a billionth of a billionth the size of an atom, which is smaller even than that little popcorn husk that gets stuck in your back tooth while watching Ben Affleck movies, then uncertainty rules. The point is, the bedrock of the material world is not bedrock at all. It's more like a waterbed, a weird

41

indeterminant plasma state. But there's a difference between uncertainty, and Wheeler's thesis that we create the world by observing it.

I know to some people this doesn't sound like such a big deal, but it was a major development in the way in which smart people think about the material world. At these infinitesimal orders of magnitude, the very act of making the observation alters the particles you're observing, and so reality becomes more elusive, a moving target. Mathematically, the law reduces our description of the world to a set of probabilities, to a bunch of likelihoods, but never to a clear, unequivocal measure. And that drove Einstein up the wall. He was a determinist to the soles of his shoes, and when Bohr and Heisenberg argued that from now on, reality at its most fundamental level will never be much more that a bundle of probabilities, Einstein actually cancelled his subscription to Bohr's Newsletter.

Of course, that incident didn't get into the papers. The famous quote that made the text books was, "God does not play dice with the universe." To which Bohr responded by pointing to Mariah Cary as proof that God is constantly playing dice with the cosmos. Einstein argued over the probabilistic nature of quantum theory for a long time; Bohr stating that reality was simply too slippery a thing to be contained by whole numbers. Probabilities were as good as we could do. "We play the percentages," he said. Einstein countered by saying the theory must be incomplete; that Quantum Theory was missing something. "At a billionth of a billionth of a billionth the size of an atom, maybe something slipped by," he said, hopefully. Since then, of course, the infinitesimal world of quantum mechanics has become weirder and weirder – including things like:

Entanglement:
If two particles called A & B are "entangled" and you change A, then B changes instantaneously, even if B is located in another state, like Oklahoma. (This is impossible. It breaks all the laws of physics.)

Super-Position:
This is a reality state in which all particles are in all places and move along all paths, all at once. (Again, impossible.)

Wave/Particle Complementarity:
This is where a particle can be a particle AND a wave at the same time, no problem. Since most people I know are two or even three things at once, I'm going to let this pass. But it's still weird.

ORIGINS
Plus, we have no explanation for the beginning of the universe, the beginning of life, or the nature of human consciousness. We have some guesses, but nothing that would hold up as a Jeopardy question.

So, this is why Einstein's hair looked that way. And yet QM, has led to extraordinarily concrete, and verifiable predictions, like how far to the Sepulveda off-ramp (GPS); the precise time of the Big Bang (Atomic Clocks) (Three-fifteen PM, Pacific, btw); and why my back always hurts (MRI). None of this would have been possible without Quantum Physics, and yet none of it makes any sense whatsoever.

While Sue is trying to wrap the Larb Gai in a most delicate envelope of fresh butter lettuce, I read that statement to her again, this time a little louder, all particles are in all places and move along all paths, all at once. That's impossible, goddamn it! At first the people at the next table were nodding, yes, but that's because they were afraid. Without moving a single sub-atomic particle in her body, for fear she would drop the Larb, Sue's eyes look at me as if to say, I can either get the Larb Gai into this little butter lettuce taco, or I can comment on superposition, but I can't do both.

I turned to the people at the next table and calmly said, "I mean haven't you ever heard about two things cannot occupy the same space at the same time? It can't be done. Right?" The man calls for his waiter. Sue creases the wings of the lettuce taco so it becomes a small modern sculpture. "And yet it's being done all day long. That damn taco is a perfect example. Look at that! It's beautiful. A miracle!"

And recently, John Wheeler has come along to speculate even further about this strange sub-sub-atomic world, and how the physical ground of our material existence may simply forever be a little out of reach. The point about quantum theory is that before we look, there is simply no way to describe the exact state of things. We can guess. We can assign probabilities. But looking shakes things up and changes them. What the world might be like in the complete absence of an observer becomes too mysterious to think about without a schooner of beer; as if seeing were a formative factor in the creation of "reality."

And I think this is what led John Wheeler to say that maybe the world does not "really" exist independent of our observation of it. Here's the quote:

"The universe may be a self-excited circuit, made real by observation."

So, me and my team are going, like, huh? Wait a minute: these guys, the greatest scientific and philosophical minds in the land, don't seem to know what the "Schubert" they are talking about. These guys have ID's that allow them into the faculty lounge at Princeton, and I mean they haven't even figured out for sure whether reality exists apart from our peering at it – I mean I don't want to get sordid, but this sounds to me a little like a form of scientific voyeurism, which is a crime in some states. And even if reality does exist, there are absolute limits to anyone's ability to describe it. It's just "uncertain." Sue raises the Larb Gai sculpture to her mouth. The lights dim. A spotlight illuminates her angelic face as she takes a first delicate bite.

Which brings us to our Christmas wish. We are not "certain." We're guessing. Even the things we feel certain about, like donuts, are uncertain. As Sue begins to chew without appearing to, she nods her head. At bottom, it's an inscrutable mystery, because there is no bottom. And if the very stuff out of which we are all made remains a deep and perhaps unfathomable mystery, then our judgments about each other, about our neighbors and colleagues and yes, even about those people who feel a stubborn obligation to blow us up, must be at least provisional.

My guys – who, as I said, only work part time – have concluded that our knowledge about things is pretty good, we're pretty smart in general. After all, we split the atom and invented the pop-top. But at bottom our particles, the things out of which we are made, remain a mystery. And that's a good thing. We thank God, whoever she is, for that. Because out of that mystery, out of that graceful limit to our understanding, flows our imagination, our artistry, our intelligence, and our best fart jokes. Because of this deep mystery of existence, David Eckstein was able to play in the majors for years without a strike zone. The two Christmas trees standing before me have become a transcendent, numinous presence in the room, all because I am observing them like crazy, and also because of the divine limits of our knowing. It reminds me of the gifts that have come to me like, "out of nowhere:" Sue Sommer, Lara and Penny being the most precious; And the love and goodwill we have felt from friends and family being the most inspiring. Finally, it is out of this same deep mystery that flows the possibility, no: the probability of change. Clearly, things are not "fixed." They may be "probable;" they may be "likely" but they are not destined. Because where uncertainty rules, there is always room for forgiveness; there's always room for the love that Jesus made the foundation of his message to the world and ground zero of our Christmas. It is a viable thing from a mysterious source, and we hope you all experience it deeply in your lives, in front of your trees, on the way to school with the kids and at your next audition.

With all our love,

Sue, Mark & Lara

2002
Important Events

- **Queen Elizabeth II celebrates her Golden Jubilee.**
  Sue celebrates by serving peas with her garlic mashed potatoes.

- **Enron Collapsed (December 2001).**
  California runs out of energy.

- **Gray Davis ends "energy" emergency in California, leaving us $34B in the red.**
  Sue absorbs cost of holiday cookies for inmates in her jails.

- **Anaheim Angels win World Series.**
  Sue considers switching allegiance from hometown Cleveland Indians to Angels. After talking to her father's ghost, however, changes mind.

- **First case of SARS, a coronavirus, recorded in Guangdong, China.**
  Peggy Lee dies. Cause of death may or may not have involved FEVER.

- **Continuing a two-year decline, the Dow lost 16.76%, closed at 8,342.**
  Lara asks, "Is this what the "new" Millennium is going to be like?

2004

Learner's Permit

(2003 Preempted by War.)

Mark, Sue & Lara Mendizza
Orange County, California

December 25, 2004

Dear Friends, Relatives and those awaiting Trial;

Of the two seasons we have here in Southern California – Warm and Warmer – I like Warm the best. We jokingly call it Fall, but California is by law an evergreen state and the only thing that falls during Fall is the price for parking at the beach. Warmer runs from about June to September, and then Warm comes and lasts from October to April. May is the wild, unpredictable period that gives our local T.V. weather people a real problem because their Doppler technology is unable to say for sure whether it's going to be warm or warmer. There's also a requirement here in this state that the I.Q. for weather people not exceed the temperatures they are forecasting, and so when Warm comes, most of them don't know how to work the Doppler anyway. But that's May. And this is either November or December (I'm not sure which), and it's totally warm outside and I just love it.

As always, the sun comes out and God sets the thermostat at a comfortable seventy-two degrees, and then adds the seasonal bonus in the form of a graceful breeze from the Pacific Ocean (which we call "the beach") to cool our faces and calm our frenzied minds as we begin once again to address the great challenges of Warm. The first challenge is thinking up a good costume for Halloween. The choice is always between "scary" or "clever," and my choice this year for scary was a Dick Cheney outfit, beige slacks and a blue blazer. But Sue said Cheney would be too scary. "A short, round, middle-aged bald guy can be a pretty terrifying thing for a young person," she said, as I stood up real straight, sucked in my ab and ran a finger through one of my several hairs. "And besides," she and Lara snickered, "you already look like Dick Cheney."

That hurt, but since reading this new book called *The Idiot's Guide to Emotional Mastery,* I've learned how to absorb errant, unfounded insults like that and to just move on with my life to the next insult. The "clever" choice was a Martha Stewart jailhouse jumpsuit, which she had converted into a line of bright orange eveningwear. As you know, Sue is in charge of all the educational programs that Santa Ana College provides to inmates at the city jail. She offers classes like, "There is NO Escape 1A," "Using Windows XT to Calculate Hard Time" and "Chicken Soup for the Criminally Insane," all of which prepare inmates to return to prison soon after they are let out. Since Sue can get free jumpsuits, we decided to go with the Martha idea.

After Halloween, comes the planning for Lara's fifteenth birthday party. Fifteen! What happened to ten? Where did nine go? Time is a devil and a saint, a mysterious, ethereal and relentless thing that just sweeps our kids along like a rap song, towards a destiny that seems less and less to require a sack lunch, good advice or even the presence of us, me, parents. Fortunately, we're all too frazzled trying to keep up with it to notice the precious things that time is taking away, like reading *Curious George* together and watching their awe arise from the simple things like swallows nesting in our eaves, instead of the Simpson sisters.

But you can't hold on to things. Like the hair on my head, the strength in my legs, the wind in my lungs, the ability to run fast, see far and think hard thoughts, you gotta let 'em go. At first she told us she just wanted something simple, maybe invite a few girlfriends to a movie and frankly I thought that was a great idea. Since she is an only child, previous celebrations usually involved a lot of strategic planning (like the year we took all the kids into outer space; that was hard), and a budget to rival what Disney spends on its Electric Light Parade. So, a few movie tickets seemed like a windfall from the parent's patron saint, known the world over as St. Bank. Then, at the last minute, she realized the consequences of her decision (which we'd been talking about to no avail for years): a "few" friends meant a "few" presents. So, nimbly as a surfer on a cresting wave, Lara changed her direction and decided she had to invite every teenage girl in the state of California.

After the party on November 21, we were immediately faced with the next big challenge with which I am sure you are all familiar: what kind of turkey to get for Thanksgiving. It posed the perennial moral choice between the Butterball, which is the kind of turkey Scott Peterson always bought, and the ethically advanced but more expensive free-range bird, which conjured up satisfying moral images of wild mustangs galloping across the wide open plains, only they're not mustangs, they're turkeys. "But Butterballs taste so much better," reasoned Sue and Lara from a lofty moral position. And so, together, as a family, we worked out a moral compromise. "OK. Let's get the butterball for Thanksgiving and from now on we'll buy nothing but those brown free-range eggs in the unbleached cardboard cartons. Does that work for everyone?"

And finally, there was the biggest challenge of all: how to prepare for the happiest and most highly anticipated event of the season: that's right, my brother's birthday. Poor Mike had the bad fortune to be born on December 6th, and that has always presented an enormous challenge to our family. As much as we would all like to, we can't just ignore it. But after all we've been through since Halloween, and with Pearl Harbor Day just a day away, and of course Christmas glistening on the horizon, the challenge has always been not to completely ignore Mike's birthday, but to find a fun and meaningful way to minimize it; like calling real early in the morning when you know he won't answer and singing happy birthday into his answering machine. That's what we usually do, but this year we innovated further and sent him birthday greetings telepathically; while doing the breakfast dishes we just stood there at the sink and thought about him real hard and through the spiritual ether that binds us all we broadcast our love and affection right up to Ojai where he lives in a small cottage nestled inside a grove of orange trees, meditating daily on the healing power of innocence and forgiveness, especially for people who get screwed out of their birthday by its cruel proximity to Christmas. He said he received our birthday vibes, and felt our love. "Better than the early morning phone call," he wept emotionally.

So here we are: The leaves are shimmering in the fierce Santa Ana winds. The air is clear as just washed windows. The hard edges of Warmer have been softened from that harsh, polluted feeling into a cozy kind of southern California clarity. It's like the major challenges of Warm have almost been met; like the hydro-carbonated haze of Warmer has lifted and before our watery eyes once again is a future that glistens with the promise of Christmas, just like the evergreens Sue and Lara finished decorating, with a star above one and our guardian angel above the other. With only one major challenge left before Santa arrives, we feel buoyed by a kind of divine dependability, knowing that no matter what the Republicans decide to do about the Empire, democracy in the Middle East, nuclear weapons in the hands of mad, avenging Muslim terrorists and of course preserving my Social Security, the temperatures here in Southern California will stay in the mid-seventies, the ocean tides will continue to ebb and flow like the tides of life itself, and there will always be plenty of sports figures and movie stars we can look to for the solace of inane, but indispensable distraction. There is just no place like Southern California, especially for avoiding reality, which is why we will always be a blue state and hopefully, if the secession thing works out, a blue nation. As Santa begins to load up his sleigh with toys for young and old, there is just one thing left for us to do, and that, as I am sure you know, is to write the annual Christmas Letter.

Ha! Fooled you, didn't I? You probably thought this WAS the Christmas Letter. In your sugarplum, whiskey-soaked eggnog dreams, perhaps. No. What you have just read is the brief introduction to the Christmas Letter, a sort of warm up, a Preamble, a loosening of the linguistic limbs so to speak, in anticipation of the long distance run that is the story of our life over the past year. I mean that's what a Christmas Letter is all about, right? Sharing our lives with your life, not something that can possibly be done in a brief note or even a two-pager. It's actually our last big challenge of the season: how to fit all the things our family has done, felt, and thought into just a few hundred pages. It's not easy, but things worth doing are never easy, are they? And sharing is SO important. And the journey of a thousand miles begins with the first step, right? Yes? Hello? You still there? Anybody?

Broadway Karma

Man, were we sick! It was December 26th, 2003, just about a year ago. Christmas was over and we couldn't remember a thing we had done or a gift we'd given or received, except Lara and I had both gotten iPODs and we planned to listen to them during the entire flight from L.A. to New York City; she to toxic teen pop rock and me to polyphonic liturgical music from the Italian and Northern Renaissance, or maybe late Metallica from Detroit. It was about three o'clock in the morning, cold, cold moonless morning and clear, probably like it was 2000 years ago in Bethlehem the day after the wise men and farm animals had given praise to baby Jesus. The big event was over, the promise of a new kind of life on earth had been made and now the hard part had begun: the Wise Men were packing for the trip home and figuring out a way of living up to the promise.

Dressed like Russians under a winter siege, we were rolling our luggage down the street to the Vann's house. Jimmy, Diane and Chelsea are our good friends and neighbors. They were the first people I ever knew who were able to actually make a living doing the things they loved to do: being prison guards. NO! I'm kidding. They're artists. They make music. I used to believe music just appeared out of nowhere, something that was just there, like nature and beer; not something made like cars and and Swiss Army knives, but a thing as natural as sunlight. People like Mozart never seemed real to me. I mean I know he existed, I saw Amadeus, but I had never really imagined him sitting down at the table and writing six hundred symphonies by the time he was nine. I still can't imagine it, dipping his little stylus into the ink jar and scribbling out all the notes to La Boheme.

It only became real to me when I watched Diane and Jimmy actually do it, compose and sing and form jazz combos and choral groups and have parties that were attended by people who knew all the words to Les Miserable. And then we saw them teach Chelsea, their beautiful daughter, to make similar music, to sing and dance and cause people to stand up and applaud. "You mean you people actually do this every day?" I asked. "For food? Like Mozart?" I don't know if they know it, but when we moved in next door to Jimmy, Diane and Chelsea, our lives changed; our imaginations expanded. That may sound intangible and hard to convert to dollars and cents (although we're trying to do that), but people aren't much more than what they're able to imagine and by expanding our vision of things, they expanded our lives. We don't want to tell them about this because they might want to charge us for it, but it did happen and we're pretty grateful. But that wasn't the big thing the Vanns did for us; the big thing was much bigger than transforming our lives, much more precious and valuable and rare: the big thing was they added a family to the neighborhood carpool.

Throats raw, heads soaked with snot, an ache that seemed almost mystical the way it spread throughout the body like an ethereal vapor of pain; Sue, Lara and I wheeled our Hartmans down to the Vann's to meet up with them and wait for the shuttle to LAX. Lara had been infected for a month or more, probably from all that time she spent at the theater. She and Chelsea had worked right up to Christmas on a show at the Laguna Playhouse, which is not only one of the finest theaters in America, but also an experimental lab for breeding new forms of infectious disease for the federal government. Sue had been in bed for five days, too, often attempting heroically to rise and revive her 16-hour-a-day routine, but quickly falling back down again like Garbo in Camille. I myself had plague and cholera, and doubts about this trip were inevitable. "We probably won't go," I had said, looking through the pantry for the hemlock. "It's just too much. The Christmas season is just too much for us." "I know," said Sue, pouring the deadly elixir down drain. "But we can't disappoint Lara."

NOTE: Ha! Fooled you again. I know Mozart didn't write La Boheme. I mean everybody knows Leonard Bernstein wrote that one, right after he did *Showboat*.

Jimmy, Diane and Chelsea towed their luggage out to the curb where we were waiting. The Star of Bethlehem was still oddly shining overhead, and I thought about the wise men on the day after Christmas, making their way back to their kingdoms, pondering the events of the night before and wondering when antibiotics would be invented. The Vanns were getting over a bad case of E. Coli and Hodgkin's Disease. When I asked Jimmy how he felt, he said, "posthumous." I didn't know what that meant, but I knew it was bad. "Why are we doing this?" I asked. And while Jimmy negotiated with the driver for a deeply discounted fare to the airport, Diane answered my question, "We don't want to disappoint Chelsea," she said.

We looked pretty weird on the plane; four adults and two kids side-by-side in the center row, all wearing a little surgical mask the color of spearmint mouthwash. When the people across the aisle looked at us, they asked if they could take another plane, "to a different continent, please," they added. But once the wheels were up and our headphones were in place, an extraordinary thing happened: we began to feel better. It may have been a miraculous healing from the renaissance polyphonic liturgical music playing on my new iPod, or it could have been the Star of Bethlehem that had been looming mysteriously above our house, or maybe it was the sixteen Sudafed I'd taken, but I remember turning to Sue and lifting the gauzy cloth away from my mouth and hardly believing my own words as I said, "I feel well." Sue's wide beautiful eyes widened even more and she lifted her gauze and responded, "I do, too. I don't feel the least bit sick." Then she turned and dealt Lara her first hand of UNO.

By the time we landed at JFK, our fevers had lifted and our spirits, though not exactly soaring, were flapping their wings really hard. While Jimmy was out in the busy street by the airport flagging down a van and negotiating another deeply discounted fare for the ride to Manhattan, Chelsea and Lara, Diane, Sue and I wheeled the luggage out of the terminal and felt the brisk arctic wind take the first layer of skin off our faces. Ahh! New York, New York. Poor Sanchez, the driver, was shivering as he listened to Jimmy explain why he needed to cut a few more points off the fare. I forgot to mention that people fortunate enough to make a living doing the things they love to do, like playing jazz piano in night clubs and producing musicals by Stephan Sondheim, don't make as much money as people who do things they hate, like selling chalk. So artistic people have to be hard negotiators, and Jimmy's one of the best. He negotiates the price of socks at Nordstrom's. He negotiates the price of gift wrap with little kids trying to raise money for their schools. And he really negotiates fares for vans to the airport. He told Sanchez that Lara and Chelsea were orphans from the Columbian drug wars, and we were returning them to their only living relatives in Manhattan, at a hotel near Broadway and 42nd street. "You must be a musician," said Sanchez, a small savvy man with a big black mustache, himself on the run from a drug cartel. "Musicians I take for free. Get in."

Soon we were looking at the New York skyline and listening to Sanchez tell Lara and Chelsea about the history of the city. "New York was founded by Columbians," he began. "It's a big rock, it's built on a big granite rock. Over there, the Africans live, and there the Asians; over there the Puerto Ricans, the Cubans, the Russians, the Ubekistanis, the Croatians, Rumanians, and Sikhs. Everybody comes here to live the American dream (pause) ... and sell designer handbags on the sidewalk ..." Then he paused, "Ground Zero is big hole. Very quiet. Very strange.

People are crazy."

We had taken Lara to New York several years ago, but it was a different world then; a bull market eight years running, a possibility of peace in the Middle East, and the Twin Towers were still a part of the Manhattan skyline. The last time we were here we all went up to the top where you could almost see the curve of the earth. Today, we planned to visit Ground Zero, but with some pause. I'm tempted to say it was a "better" more promising world back then than it is today, though I'm not sure. There are profound limits to human knowledge and we should never be too sure of anything (Personally, my beliefs are all based on a version of Baysian Probabilty and a Ouiji Board.) But good things can still happen, even in difficult times, and there's really only one thing one can be absolutely certain about: this trip is going to take every cent we have stashed away in Lara's college fund.

The Edison Hotel is right in the middle of the theater district, 228 West 47th. Times Square is half a block away and all the theaters are within walking distance. It had been a long day since the six of us had stood together outside our houses early in the cold clear morning, holiday phlegm gurgling inside of our heads, the big Star above and memory of Christmas giving way to the anticipation of the trip to New York. Now we were in a little Italian restaurant around the corner from the Edison, crowded together at a narrow table covered with white linen. It was totally New York, cozy, colorful and diverse. We'd finished dinner and we were all talking about how fantastic the city was, especially at this time of year. I had stealthily moved the empty wicker bread basket over the little spot of olive oil I had spilled on the table, when the conversation suddenly drifted toward carpooling. Uh

Oh. To me that was a red flag. I knew we had reached a critical point in our journey. We were tired; jet lagged. Dazed not only by the long day, the long season and the long decade, but also by the overwhelming scale and infinite possibilities of the city itself. We were excited about everything, but not sure what to do about anything: call it a night, start drinking or work out bus schedules for next semester.

I remembered the discount ticket booth on Times Square where sometimes you can pick up tickets to first-rate shows for half price. It was seven-thirty at night and curtain time for most of the shows on Broadway was eight o'clock. There wasn't much chance of getting to a theater before show time, let alone reaching the booth in time to get discounted tickets. But I knew I had to do something. I knew that descending into conversation about carpooling could be fatal. "I'm thinking we take a shot," I said, "Pay the bill and run down to that discount ticket booth. It's probably too late, but what have we got to lose? I mean we're sitting here talking about carpooling. Anybody up for a show?" The girls were. They were up for anything; as ready to create a show as attend one. And eventually even the more mature individuals in the group decided a brisk jog to the discount booth was a good idea.

By the time we had lost all the feeling in our faces as we ran in the cold wind toward Broadway, it was about seven-forty. Diane had peeled off from the herd to retreat to a warm bed and resume her adventure after a night's sleep. We found the booth and we got in line, the clock ticking away, reducing our chances by the minute. Seven-fifty: we're surrounded by the mega-lights and towering, monumental urban structures of Times Square, standing in the cold, watching most of the people in the crowd begin to give up and walk away, when suddenly this guy walks up to us and raises his hand toward our faces so we can better see the six tickets he is holding for *Gypsy*, starring Bernadette Peters. It's seven fifty-five. Curtain goes up in five minutes. Undaunted, Jimmy steps up and begins to negotiate. "How many of those do you have?" he asks. "Six," says the guy, "for tonight's show. Four up front center in the orchestra, two fourth row right." "I'll give you a hundred dollars," says Jimmy. And the guy's face lights up. The tickets were worth at least a hundred and twenty dollars each, and this guy thought a hundred each was pretty good. He did not understand, of course, that Jimmy is a practicing artist. "For all of them," Jimmy added.

Now we're all running again, up Broadway through a dense Manhattan crowd toward the theater. As he jogs along, his Burberry blowing in the wind, Jimmy has his cell phone in his ear, telling Diane to put her coat back on and meet us at the theater in two minutes. We enter the theater doors just as the final warning bell begins to ring. It's warm, bustling and totally sold out. As the curtain rises on the show, all of us are pulling off our coats and lowering ourselves into our most excellent seats. It was a spectacular show and a wonderful way to end a day that began what seems like a lifetime ago. The musical is of course about the life of Gypsy Rose Lee, and as much about her mother as Gypsy herself. At one point in the show *Gypsy* removes one of her green satin garters and throws it out into the audience. At another point she removed a long, arm-length satin glove and threw it in the audience as well. Then she removed her . . . No. Kidding. She did a nice fan dance, but after all it was a family show. Afterwards, we met Lara and Chelsea in the lobby. After telling us how thrilled they were with the show, Lara said,

"Look." And showed us the garter AND the glove, both of which she had caught down there in the fourth row to the right. It was our first night in New York, and it was clear we had had the benefit of some good Broadway Karma.

One obtains Broadway Karma by doing good works in the theater, and it was easy to understand how Lara, Chelsea, Diane and Jimmy had acquired theirs. But Sue had the BEST Broadway Karma of all and yet it was kind of a mystery how she had acquired so much of it. *Hairspray* was a good example. Chelsea and Lara had been singing the songs from *Hairspray* for months during the carpooling from home to school. It was a very hot musical that they both were looking forward to seeing. Sue got tickets, but then she used some of her Karma to get backstage passes to the play, as well; which was like impossible to get. But not for Sue. That's the extraordinary thing about her; good things just come to her, with a few exceptions such as her husband. Anyway, Sue works with Stacy at the college. And many years ago Stacey used to attend the Orange County High School for the Performing Arts, just like Lara and Chelsea. Later, however, she decided to get out of the entertainment business and become an educator. She's an associate professor at Santa Ana College, but a lot of the friends she made while attending OCHSA went on to work as performers, including her friend Terron Brooks. Terron just happens to have a lead role in *Hairspray* and when Sue mentioned that we were going to be seeing the play, Stacey called Terron and got us all backstage passes. After the performance, we were back there hanging out with Terron and Matthew Morrison and all the other members of the cast (except Harvey Fierstein who didn't do guests). Since we were all chatting on the stage, both Lara and Chelsea can now say with some conviction that they've been "On the Broadway Stage." And all because of the Sue's Broadway Karma.

Teen Karma

The ancient Greeks believed the creation of teens was a punishment, not of teens themselves, but of their errant parents. In the myth, the great King Agamemdale and Queen Queen (her name was actually Queen) were childless. They'd tried all the fertility rites in the realm; wearing short togas around the house, listening to old Commodores songs and even you-know-what. But nothing worked and so they made a bargain with the gods. The gods said they would give them children—in fact, they said they would give them their children; under one condition: that the two royals promise never to have any fun or enjoyment on their own again; no movies, no dinners out, no you-know-what. King Agamemdale and Queen Queen agreed and for many years they kept their promise and didn't have any fun. They did nothing but maintenance on the realm, care for the kids and crawl into bed as soon as the royal tots were asleep. Then, just as their first-born was turning thirteen, the gods caught Dale sneaking in a few holes on the back nine and the Queen slipping into a day spa for a facial. When the gods discovered what they had done, they were, as usual, merciless. Queen Queen found Dale wailing and gnashing his teeth on the floor of the castle. "What's wrong?" she exclaimed, her face all soft and relaxed from the ancient Greek dermabrasion. "The Gods discovered our transgressions and have passed mighty judgment upon us." "Uh Oh," said Queen Queen. "Maybe they'll take the kids back." "Nay, dear Queen. Alas. The kids are kids no longer. They have been turned into teens." And parents have suffered thus ever since.

The Elizabethans believed that teenagers were possessed by devils and they hired exorcists, which they called "high school teachers," to cure them. Today, of course, we know that adolescence is actually a disease. When looked at with advanced imaging techniques such as a magnifying glass, it has been shown that during adolescence certain parts of the human brain turn into pudding. Until the brain matures and becomes mush like the parent brain, the teen is a victim of brain anatomy and cannot help saying to their parents things such as, "take me to the mall and then get out of my life." Or threats like, "If you don't get me a car and teach me how to drive I'll live in this house until I am thirty." They are also unable to clean a room or, when in the presence of important relatives with lots of inheritable money, speak words of more than one syllable, usually "no" and "yeah."

In the past, societies controlled the teen population through warfare. As illustrated in the recent movies, "Troy" and "Alexander," the teens of one society lined up by the tens of thousands on one side of a corn field and faced tens of thousands of teens from another kingdom on the other side of the field, and then killed each other with spears and axes while the parents looked on, trying desperately to withhold their smiles. Today, of course, we're more civilized. We've seen the folly of war (or at least many of our teens have) and the only teen-control methods we have left are vats of Ritalin, the iPod and of course High School, which is where we sent Lara to learn more about her disease.

OK. I've been kidding and now I want to tell you the truth, about Lara. The real Lara. Traditionally that's what the Christmas letter is for, to share information about what our kids have achieved, or if they haven't achieved anything, to make some things up that can't be verified. Once children become teens, however, it's more difficult to do because parents really have no idea what their teens are doing. They get up and go to school, and you don't see them again until they come home at night to sulk. Lara, for example gets up at 5:30. She steps out of her pajamas, which fall to the floor and remain there, and into her jeans which are right there conveniently on the floor waiting for her. She puts on some mascara, plugs her iPod into her ear, and receives a totally balanced, vitamin-rich bowl of Frosted Flakes. She is in the backseat of the car, still sound asleep at 6:30, as mommy slides into the driver's seat and takes her to school. That's all we see of her for the rest of the day. She starts her day at school at 7:00 a.m. with AP Algebra. She ends at 3:00 p.m. and goes directly to tennis practice. On Wednesday she goes to her conservatory at the Laguna Playhouse. We try to keep track of her, but it's hard. Like, "How was your day, sweetheart?" "Yeah." "Anything interesting happen?" "No." Did you know the east coast of the United States broke off and fell into the ocean today?" "No. I didn't. Well, I have to go." Then she goes into her room to do her homework, which in Lara's case means solving twenty or thirty equations such as the following:

$$2x = \{(\pi 0 + \varepsilon/\chi \ A0) - \alpha 1 \ (\pi 1 + \varepsilon/\chi \ A1 \ ) - \alpha 2 \ (\pi 2 + \varepsilon/\chi \ A2 \ ) - \alpha 3 \ (\pi 3 + \varepsilon/\chi \ A3 \ ) - \alpha \mu \ \mu \chi \ \} \ \Psi.$$

Solve for Ω using the inverse quotient of the random variable $\delta + z$, with a standard deviation of .000001 or $-i \ (\partial \mu - m \ )$, whichever is larger. Use long division. Round up. And show your work.

Of course, I have always been there to help Lara with her homework and in this case, I told her I thought the answer was four, but she better double check.

I mean I'm not kidding. I mean I am kidding about all the

teen stuff. She has a few teen characteristics, like a complete, schizophrenic break from reality, but Lara is no teen. She's a young lady, on the way to becoming a beautiful young woman, and she never stops amazing me with her deep knowingness, discriminating taste (especially for breakfast cereals) and unbounded grace under fire, all of which is not easy to carry off with a father who still thinks booger jokes are funny and gets laughs at the dinner table by making cool bodily noises.

And I'm totally not kidding about her academic load. At just fourteen and half years old Lara was taking AP European History, which is a college credit course taught by a guy who likes to scare his students with more information about the Counter Reformation than is healthy for a young person to know. She's taking AP Spanish, Honors English, Drama 2, and Honors Chemistry, a class that asks kids who don't know how to drive yet to find the error in reasoning in the following proof:

> *Proof.*—According to Newton, the number of "lines of force" which come from infinity and terminate in a mass m is proportional to the mass m. If, on the average, the mass-density P0 is constant throughout the universe, then a sphere of volume V will enclose the average mass P0V. Thus, the number of lines of force passing through the surface F of the sphere into its interior is proportional to P0V. For unit area of the surface, the number of lines of force which enters the sphere is thus proportional to $P0 \cdot v/F\}$ or P0R. Hence the intensity of the field at the surface would ultimately become infinite with increasing radius R of the sphere to six, which is impossible.

Always there with the answers, I explained to Lara that this was a trick question. The error was not with Sir Isaac Newton, it was with the Saddleback Unified School District for asking a young girl that kind of question. I mean is there no decency?

Tennis Karma

In addition to struggling with her academics and trying to determine what in this world is real and what is just being made up by adults for their own benefit, Lara also competed on the high school tennis team. That was quite an unexpected development in our lives. She had taken some tennis lessons when she was younger, but for the last several years her focus—when it was not on following Ashley Simpson's career or the plot points of a show called Alias—was on the theater, which of course is where she acquired the Broadway Karma. During her first year in high school, however, her gym teacher, Mrs. Mello, saw Lara swing a tennis racquet. She perceived a grace and follow-through that was rare and encouraged Lara to try out for the tennis team the following year. So Lara began practicing her tennis once again, hitting balls, working on her volleys and serves. Last summer she tried out and not only did she make the team, she made varsity, "sort of."

I say "sort of" because even though she had made the varsity team, she ended up playing junior varsity. It was a pretty dicey deal and I think took Lara another step into the mushy, ever-shifting real-world landscape of adult priorities, especially when it comes to organized, high school sports. Technically she competed and won a spot on the varsity team, but Lara was only a sophomore and there were several girls, juniors and seniors, who had been on the team for a few years and who had parents who, if their girl's spot were to be given to Lara, would have declared a soccer-mom Jihad on the coach. His life on the line, coach explained to Lara that if she played varsity she would be at the bottom of the roster and if she played J.V. she would be at the top. "You'll play much more on the JV team," he pointed out, "plus they won't burn down my house." There was merit to this argument, but still, Lara had won a spot on varsity and wanted the damn varsity jacket that went with the spot. It was a very difficult compromise for her, but at the end of the season, playing J.V. was probably the best thing that could have happened.

It was a Thursday afternoon and I was driving to Beverly Hills to get my hair cut and see my analyst. I go there a month or so to visit with my unconscious mind and learn about the celebrity-of-the-month from Domingo, the guy who cuts my hair. During my analysis, my analyst says, "There are only a handful of marriages that are really working these days, or at least that I know of: yours, my daughter's and a few others." I thought that was interesting. Sue and I do still love one another, even though our lives are stretched too thin by the complexities of work, raising a teen and being old. So if you're married and you still love the person you are married to and can take a walk or go to a movie and still hold hands and feel like two birds sitting on a fence in the warm summer sun, then hold on to that. It's possible you'll be on T.V. someday.

As I walked out of her office, my cell phone rang. It's Sue. She's at Lara's tennis match, hiding behind a tree, watching Lara compete. Lara is the only member of her team to have advanced to the league finals where she is competing for first place in the singles category. During the season she beat just about everybody she played, except for three girls from I think Dana High

School who have been bred since birth to beat kids who don't go to Dana. And they've done it. They feed on the flesh of their opponents. They do nothing but practice tennis and they beat everyone. Lara's playing the number one seeded player and she's getting killed. "I don't think she's scored a point yet," whispers Sue, who Lara will not allow to observe the game, "but she's playing beautifully." We are just so proud of her out there. This is what I mean by grace under pressure. She's shown it over and over again in the theater, with those math problems that Einstein gave up on, and now on the tennis court. I feel guilty about not being there, but the celebrity-of-the-month is Soupy Sales, and I know Sue will keep me informed.

OK, I'm sitting in the chair, and Domingo is cutting what few hairs I have left, saying things like, "I think you have a lot more than Dick Cheney." He begins to tell me some seedy stories about the Beverly Hill celebrities when my cell rings again. I answer it. "She got beat pretty bad," reports Sue. "But she played so well. This girl was just unbeatable." "That's great," I said. "She's come so much further than we ever thought she would. I mean this is her first time ever to really compete like this." "I know. Now she's playing the other girl for third place, singles. I gotta go. I'll call you back."

This is almost impossible to believe. If you've ever seen Lara you know she is very petite, and to be honest, she's not as fully developed physically as a lot of high school girls I've seen, especially these older girls from Dana High who as infants were found in baskets floating down the L.A River. After my hair cut I walk over to a little chocolatier called Teuscher's and sit down at a sidewalk table to sip a cappuccino and watch all the beautiful people who are walking by. Most of the them are saying "Ciao!

Hey Ciao. Yeah, Ciao to you, too. Ciao, baby." I'm getting ready to say "chow" to the next person that walks by when the phone rings again. "She's up 4-3," Sue whispers with an excitement that actually rattles the table. "But the coach just got mad at her for hitting a ball that would have gone out." And then Sue tells me about the mother of Lara's opponent. "She is absolutely furious," she said. "She's over there just fuming about Lara moving ahead of her daughter. "All three of these girls beat that girl last time," she kept saying about Lara. "How can this be happening? What is going on?" What is going on is that Lara is finding her center. She has gradually found her poise and is keeping the ball in play. Sometimes that's the key to success, just keeping the ball in play. Now I am really getting excited, too. The possibility that Lara could beat one of these feral girls and win third place singles in the whole league has just been a very remote possibility. But now, here it is. Within reach. And the great thing, the most wonderful thing is that the opponent's mother, who was giving illegal cues to her daughter, got her finger caught in the chain-link fence.

I have to drive to Westwood to meet my sister and I'm in the car when the next call comes in. "She just played a game that lasted fifteen minutes, I mean these two girls batted the ball back and forth for fifteen minutes, and Lara won. She's up 5-3." Oh my god! "Coach is right here with her, talking to her." "Is it helping?" I asked. "Yes. Lara is listening to him and making corrections." I'm a little sad at that. She hardly ever listens to me, but then I'm a Dad and coach is coach.

There's a Farmer's Market going on in Westwood and it's hard to find a parking place. I drive around in the heavy UCLA traffic and finally see an empty space not too far from a little stand that's selling Brazilian food. I begin thinking about moving to Brazil. It's dusk, the darkness is softening the hard, urban edges and I realize that Lara has been competing since one o'clock in the afternoon, over five hours on the court; battling girls that make Zena look like a Barbie doll. As I pull into my space, the cell phone rings. I maneuver my car into place and stop, turn off the engine, press talk and raise the phone to my ear. "This is Mark," I say, pretending to be important. At first there's a silence. A long pause. "Hello," I repeat. "Dad?" It's Lara. My heart is in my throat. I love her so much! I don't care whatsoever whether she had won or lost this game, but I can't help it; either way, something important is at stake here, something important has happened today and the tension is like a rubber band stretched to its limit, either it breaks or takes off. "Yes, honey. Yes. How are you? How did it go? Another long pause. "I won," she says.

Later in the month, Lara was awarded her medal for third place singles in the league and voted the Most Valuable Player by her team and coaches.

The Karma of Conversation

As I pointed out, Sue and I don't have many opportunities to really talk with Lara because she is SO busy figuring out new ways to avoid us. She figures if she takes another class or gets another role in a play that's just one less conversation she will have to have with her parents about her life, plans for college and what she did at school on any given day, which of course was "nothing." By accident, however, we have stumbled into a few exchanges that went beyond a "yes" or "no" answer. Like back in September I remember having one.

73

It was fairly late at night. School books and supplies were stacked up on the floor of the office like a strange geological formation and after Mommy went to bed, Lara and I remained in front of the computer discussing the essay on nature she was going to have to compose for her new honors English class. I love talking to her about her schoolwork, even though I got her in trouble when I explained that the reformation is a technical word for fashion make-over. We were talking about the nature of humankind and I was pointing out how unique our species was.

Dad: But no other creature in nature has been able to make tools, develop agriculture or split the atom.

Lara: Why do we need to split the atom?

Dad: Huh?

Lara: Why do we need to split the atom? All this technology and stuff is just destroying nature, not helping it.

Dad: Yeah, but . . .

Lara: Even all the medicines that are used to cure cancer and keep people alive so long. Why are we doing that?"

Dad: I don't know. Because it seems like the right thing to do, to stop suffering.

Lara: Yes. True. But is longevity the goal of life, then, to just see who can live the longest?

Dad: Of course not. The goal is to . . . well . . . abstain from sex and get into a good college.

Lara: Right, Dad.

Dad: What are we supposed to do? Just let them die?

Lara: Of course not. But if the people were just allowed to die, if nature was allowed to just follow its course, then the genes that make cancer would eventually also die, wouldn't they? I mean they would not be passed along to the next generation and we would eventually be free of the disease.

Dad: Who have you been talking to young lady. I mean you're right. It's true. By helping the very weak and the sick to survive we are kind of going against the laws of evolution. But those are the arguments the Nazis used to kill the Jews. They said they were inferior people and should be exterminated to create a stronger more evolved race. I mean we can't just let people who are sick die, can we?"

Lara: I don't mean that.

Dad: I know. But you better get clearer on your argument.

Lara: I mean the dolphins haven't split the atom and they live a wonderful life, if we would just stop killing them with our nets and sonar.

Dad: Ah well, that's what you mean. That we should lead more natural lives.

Lara: Yes. Why do we need all this technology?

Dad: To make life and survival easier, so we can watch more T.V. and make more discriminating purchases.

Lara: But is it really easier? Aren't we destroying the earth, polluting the air and water?

Dad: Maybe we are, honey, but I think it's time for bed, don't you?

This is another thing about teens. First you can't get them to talk, but then once you do they start asking all these difficult questions, without understanding how much our lifestyle depends on 3% to 5% economic growth per day, no matter what happens to the dolphins. I think I helped her understand the adult perspective, though, which is something a parent is supposed to do.

Then there was this other conversation in March we had about the origins of "front" and "rear." I know. It didn't make sense to me at first either, but think about it. "Front" and "Rear" have a history. We were reading Lara's biology text and discovered this weird point in the evolution of animal life when there was no "front" or "back" or side or anything like direction. This is a little complicated and some of you may want to skip this part and just go on to where I describe my mother's double by-pass heart surgery, which took place last February. When your primordial family ancestors had just barely reached the point where they had more than one cell—fortunately for us, our family has apparently always had at least two or three cells—but when your ancestors were barely a multi-celled organism, with no eyes or feet or hands or even brains, we – I mean your family – had no concept of front or back, forward or backward. So whenever somebody would say, "I'm moving forward with my life," nobody would have the slightest ideas what they were talking about."

Dad: You mean we were just shapeless, amorphous creatures?

Lara: Exactly, Dad. We were like drops of water. Do drops of water have a front? No. That's how we were.

Dad: Then how did we figure out "front?"

Lara: Light. We evolved cells inside of our little Jello bodies that became just slightly sensitive to light.

Dad: And that was front?

Lara: No. But that was the beginning of eyes, which was the beginning of front.

Dad: Whoa. Is that cool?

Lara: Over millions of years the organism discovered that moving toward light helped it survive, and so the cells that were light sensitive increased through natural selection and began to gather in one location in the body. After another million years, the organism could move up close to a rock and stick its light sensitive cells a little bit forward and almost sense what was around the corner.

Dad: That's like the beginning of "seeing."

Lara: Right!

Dad: And that helped us survive, too, right? Because it could see its enemies before they saw it.

Lara: Right. That was the beginning of eyes. The organism was evolving a "front."

Dad: So "front" didn't always exist, did it?

Lara: There was a time when there was no such thing as "Front." "Front" evolved.

Dad: And "Rear?"

Lara: Rear evolved, too, Dad. But I don't want to talk about that.

And then sometimes Lara seems more like the parent than

the parent. I don't know how this happened. I can remember when she was just a few months old and unable to stop crying or sleep, and in the middle of the night I would put her into the car seat of the old blue Volvo we used to have and I'd drive south toward Mexico. While driving mile after mile I would sing songs and with her little infant fist Lara would stare into the night, rock back and forth in her car seat and hold on to my finger until she fell asleep. Today, which seems like just a few weeks later, she's telling me what to do. Like I remember leaving an important meeting one afternoon to rush home and take Lara to her orthodontist appointment. While driving toward the house, I called her to confirm our schedules.

> Dad: Hi honey, I'm coming up the hill to take you to the orthodontist.
> Lara: That's tomorrow, Dad.
> Dad: Huh? Tomorrow! Are you sure?
> Lara: It's tomorrow, Dad
> Dad: Tomorrow. I thought it was today. Tomorrow you go to your teen brain enhancement clinic and so I thought today was the Orthodontist.
> Lara: No. Both are tomorrow.
> Dad: Well, shoot. What do I do?
> Lara: Go back down the hill. I'm singing.

It may seem strange, but Lara never seems to want us around, especially when she sings. In fact, when she is eating or reading or while she's taking in air and exhaling she doesn't really like having her parents lurking around either. But I know she loves me. I can tell because you know what she gave me for my birthday? She gave me a fossil of the Orthoceras, a long straight cephalopod from the Devonian Period, which lived over 350 million years ago. The cephalopod of course was one of the first creatures in our family to develop a "front."

Trip Karma

As I mentioned, since she all of a sudden grew up, Sue and I don't see or talk much to Lara any more. She's either going to school, practicing tennis, working on her acting, doing IM'ing on the computer, hanging out with friends or inventing new and interesting ways to avoid us altogether. So when there's a break in the schedule, we try to take trips and that gives us a chance to interrogate, . . . er, I mean communicate with her. . Like I think it was last July we all went up to a little cabin on Lake George in Mammoth.

We wanted to leave at ten in the morning, but each year we want to leave at ten and we never pull out of the driveway until twelve. This year was no different. It's one of Newton's laws, one of nature's immutable principles that govern the stars, planets and family vacations. True departure time (TDT) is intended departure time (IDT), plus two hours (IDT+2=TDT). You can actually graph it out year after year and create your own family equation, or give it to your teen for homework. There's just always one more thing to do before you can actually leave.

Send more e-mails
Decide again which book to take
Put more shirts into luggage
Should really go to the gym first

Cut up celery sticks and carrots and put in cooler with
    Krispie Kremes
Send more e-mails
Charge the cell phone
Put the rolodex into the suitcase
Write a note to the neighbors thanking them for picking
    up mail and defending house against local teens while
    we are gone
One more email

When we finally backed out of the driveway at twelve thirty and accelerated down our long neighborhood street, we experienced that faint ecstatic sensation that comes when a family leaves its dull, tedious, "to-do-ridden" life behind and launches out into something that resembles the "unknown."

But wait! We're cruising down the residential street on the way, if not to the "great," then at least to the "relative" unknown, when I turn to Sue and alertly say, "Did you bring the phone number to the lodge?" "No," Sue responded with a slight edge, preparing to defend herself against impending attacks on her skills as a vacation partner. "Do we need it?" "No. I don't think so. Let's just go." "Yeah. Let's just go." "That's what we're going to do. We're just going to go."

We turned left and continued another hundred yards on our great adventure where the freedom of the great outdoors would replace the tyranny of 3% to 4% net annual growth. "What about the recipe for the re-baked potatoes?" I asked. The night before, Lara had called from Nana's place where she had spent the night, and asked if we had packed the recipe for the re-baked potatoes. "And could you make sure to put a pillow and a blanket into the back seat for me, and a box of Triscuits," she reminded us for the sixth time. "No," replied Sue once again. "But I think I remember the ingredients. Potatoes, I think." "Good. Good. Then let's just go, right?" "Right," "OK. We're on our way. "Yup. Here we go. Another excursion into the wild world of the relative unknown." "Off we go."

Another half mile and then, "Ahh. What about the European history book? Did we bring Lara's European history textbook?" Lara is enrolled in this very demanding AP, college level history course next year where she will be asked to remember words like Baroque. Sue and I had actually gone to the school and asked them if we could check out the textbook during the summer so that Lara could preview the word before the new school year began in September. Do you think that's too extreme? Do you think we're out of our minds? OK. Now I detect a change in Sue's tone. Re-baked potatoes are one thing. Lara's history book is something else, because Lara's ability to remember the word "Baroque" and paraphrase the meaning of David Hume's "Treatise on Human Understanding" is directly related to which college she will be admitted to and that is directly related to what kind of career she will have, which has a direct correlation to the type of boy she will meet, which is directly related to the type of private detective we will have to hire to investigate the unscrupulous, sex-crazed retard who thinks he's good enough to marry our daughter.

"Didn't we bring the history book?" she asks, with a new tension in her voice. "I placed it in the pile at the top of the stairs." "No. That was the Chemistry book," I explained. (Ah. Well. See. Lara is also taking AP Chemistry and we thought while we were hiking up the eastern slopes of the High Sierras we could also get a jump on the Periodic Table of the Elements.) We arrived at the stoplight at the bottom of the hill, and the light was red. There was a pause. And then, as if I had just discovered the value of "x," I erupted with the word, "Flashlight! Did we bring a flashlight? I know we're going to need a flashlight! I mean if we want to survive."

I made a quick illegal U-turn and headed back home. Yes, I saw the policeman heading toward the intersection on our left, and I did hesitate. But I was already committed to the turn. The truth is, when I saw the cop, I was right in the middle of the infraction and to try to stop would have drawn more attention to the violation that continuing in a smooth, seamless way to break the law. "There's a policeman," said Sue. "It says right there, no U-turn. Now we're going to get a ticket." But no; the highway patrolman just cruised through the intersection and I headed back up the hill to get the flashlight, the text book on European history, the *Periodic Table of the Elements* and the recipe for re-baked potatoes.

Back in the car after packing the new survival stuff in the trunk, we headed out again on our spiritual journey to the land of the relative unknown. Er . . . No. Wait. Something was still missing. Where's Lara?

Right. First we had to pick Lara up at her Grandmother's. She had spent the night there and for a very strange reason. Can you guess why? I don't think so. Dog dander. The day before, Lara had been to our Korean-born, homeopathic, alternative doctor to receive some kind of chakra manipulation that was supposed to help the immune system defend itself against Penny, our dachshund; or at least against her dander. Lara has had bouts of asthma since she was two years old, and often it is related to terrible infections and allergies that only Koreans can fix. In ways this makes her achievements in school, theater and the tennis court that much more impressive; because for our dear Lara, breathing is always an issue.

Following the treatment, which I think consisted of placing needles in a very specific spot behind Lara's left heel, she could not, under any circumstances be exposed to dander or any past episodes of Friends. If she did encounter dander, the treatment, which I paid for by selling a kidney, would have been rendered ineffective. So Lara stayed the night at Grandma's, which is why she had called us to make sure we put the pillow and the blanky and the box of Triscuits in the back seat.

After realizing that Lara was not in the car with us, we hung another U-turn and headed back to Grandma's, who prefers the name Nana. Nana is over ninety years old, but that doesn't matter because she's also immortal. When you and I are looking for a good location to build in the afterlife, Nana will still be here complaining about how much it costs to live in Park Terrace, which is an assisted living facility designed specifically to take away all her life savings. She is still extremely healthy with a robust personality that makes people half her age, like me and our president for example, look a little demented by comparison.

But there are some blind spots in her worldview and some eccentricities in the way in which she perceives and understands things. She and I were talking one day about George Bush and I was trying to explain why I felt we should seek new leadership. "Let me put it this way," I explained slowly. "Let's say you had spent your entire life building up a company. You had good relationships with all your partners, your vendors and especially with all your customers. Let's say your business was doing great, but you were a little long in years and felt you needed to hire a professional manager to help you run your business. So you hire this guy, right. And three years later, your business is billions of dollars in debt, most of your customers and nearly all your partners hate your company and secretly wish you would fail. Let's say a thousand of your employees have been killed and about half of them would really like to quit. The only real friends you've got are people who either want to borrow money from you or who owe you lots of it already. Let's say your new manager believes that God has chosen him to run your company, and that God is the one who is giving your new manager all his instructions on how to run things. And then let's say that the term of his contract has run out and it's time to decide whether or not to extend his contract or look for new leadership. What would you do? Would you keep this guy as your manager or would you seek new leadership?

Nana looked at me, but didn't say a word. Just looked and made a thoughtful face. After a half-hour, I gave her another little prompt, "Would you continue to allow the manager to run your company or would you begin to look for someone else?" I think Nana may have drifted off to another mental place and my prompt brought her back. She continued to think, and finally said, "Well. I'm not sure." This surprised me of course because I had thought the answer would be obvious. I asked Nana why she wasn't sure. "Well," she said. "I don't know. What if you were related to the manager? What if he was your brother?"

Classic Nana; careening off the edge of a question into a stratospheric realm that only she knows. I mean kinship could be a factor here, but I think the reason her mind reaches out to such extreme speculation is because she just doesn't like to make decisions like the one I was asking her to make. Plus, she began to think she really DID own that business and was trying to remember what had happened to it. But the big obstacle was she didn't want to hurt GWs feelings. She just didn't want hurt him by stating right out that she might like to try another president. The way she gets around these encounters is by piling on contingencies, no matter how unlikely or impossible.

After spending the early morning hours getting her socks on, Edna mines the financial pages for that fraction of a point advantage in interest rates for her CDs, and then sets out to reduce her intake of food and oxygen so that there will be more for everyone else, especially Sue and Lara.

We pulled up in front of Park Terrace and Nana and Lara were standing under the big awning out in front, waiting for us. Sue rolled down her window and said, "Hi, honey," to Lara who was lifting her backpack onto her back. Then she looked at Nana and of course saw something that disturbed her. Her new prescription nylon support stockings that she had gotten her after the doctor had drained the fluid from her knee didn't look like they had been put on properly. "Nana, you have to pull your socks up higher," she said. "They're down too low." Nana didn't quite understand. "Your new stockings. They're too low. The doctor said you had to pull them up over your thigh. Mid-thigh." I don't think Nana quite understood the idea of mid-thigh. "Over your thigh," she said again. "If you leave it down there below your knee, you'll cut off the circulation to the rest of your leg and it will fall off." Nana points to her leg, below the knee and looks up, inquiringly. Sue says, "No. Higher." Nana raises her finger along the side of her leg to just above the knee. "Higher," says Sue. Nana's finger moves up another six inches and stops at what a normal person would consider to be mid-thigh. "There!" says Sue. "Pull them up to there." Nana smiles. Lara climbs into the back seat with her backpack, pillow and blanky. "Bye, Nana." Nana smiles and waves.

OK. That's it. Ready to head out once again into the mystery and wonder of the relatively unknown. As I leave the parking lot and pull out into traffic, Sue exclaims with a new sense of adventure and enthusiasm, "We need to stop at a drugstore so Lara can get some throat lozenges." I pull up to a stop sign and stop. "Go to Rite-Aid," says Lara. "Which way to Rite Aid?" I ask. "Or Ralphs," says Sue "Or Von's." "What about Pavillions?" I add. "Isn't Pavillions just over there?" "Pavillions IS Vons," says somebody. I'm confused. Always the clear one who pierces through the fog of parenthood, Lara says firmly "No. Just go to Rite Aid, Dad."

Planned departure time, plus three hours now. But we don't care. We know that eventually we will be face to face with the relatively unknown. Sue and I are waiting in the parking lot when Lara comes walking out, not with throat lozenges, but two big boxes of Triscuits. "I couldn't resist it," she says. "Buy one, get one free."

It took much less time to drive to Mammoth than it did to leave our house. We were surrounded by the stark steep gray mountains that formed the basin that was Lake George. It was dusk and cooling, air fresh and crisp as the ice still clinging to the crags and crevices up the slopes. As the wind whooshed through the tall pines you could hear the needles whisper and trees creak. I walked down the gravel path to the little lobby where I talked with Stan, the owner of the lodge. Among the many shelves of well-worn books and games with missing pieces I found an old copy of "The Amazing Bone," by William Steig. I walked back to the cabin and lit a little fire. Lara and Sue had unpacked, and as the fire began to warm us there was one of those big vacation pauses that back home would probably have been filled with an episode of "Everybody Loves Raymond" or some helpful nagging from Mom and Dad to Lara. But here we had nothing but the crackling fire and our wonderful, alpine boredom. I sat down on the old, old, really old sofa that had been in the cabin since statehood, and I lifted the book up so Sue and Lara could see the picture of Pearl, the little pig with the amazing bone (it talked), and I read the title, The Amazing Bone. Then I turned each page and showed them the picture and read the story very slowly, savoring the words and each exquisite image (Steig was a very cool illustrator as well as writer). It was a very special moment in our lives, because it was so totally unexpected and so relatively unknown. By the time we were finished with the Bone, we weren't bored any more. We were . . . well let's say content and just a little amazed ourselves at how amazing it was to be amazed together like this.

We hiked the mountains during the day. To prove to Sue and Lara I was still worthy, I jumped into the ice cold lakes and swam until the rangers came and pulled me out. At night we played Scrabble, where Lara tried to convince us that OOGPLODNZ was a word. We played her favorite game, "Get That Bug!" a lot, too. In that game we took turns searching for the bug that was either biting her at the moment or that was in hiding until bedtime when it would begin its feast. Lara also began her first driving lessons up there in Mammoth. We practiced in a big empty parking lot by a school. She loved the entire experience, driving around in circles, turning right, turning left, pulling into parking spaces, then pulling out again. But the thing she loved the most was the U-turn. The little Mercedes turns on a dime and she just whirled the vehicle around in quick, exhilarating one-hundred-and-eighty-degree turns that was "Just SO much FUN."

While circling the parking lot Sue said, "I never had much of a desire to drive. I don't think I got my driver's license until I was eighteen." This shocked Lara and caused her to drive the car into the school auditorium. "What!" she said. "How could you NOT get a license the minute you turned sixteen?" For a teen, at least a southern California teen, a car is THE right of passage, the place where a young person grows up and learns to take responsibility for getting their parents to pay for their gas and insurance.

"I rode my bike," Sue replied. "I was out on my bike all the time, just riding around, looking for butterflies. I never felt the need for a car." And knowing Sue, I was certain she wasn't exaggerating. "Mommy is very unique," I remarked. "It's the difference between growing up in the Ohio and growing up in Southern California. I bet if you went back to Ohio where Mommy came from you'd still find all kinds of people riding around on their bikes at eighteen years old, looking for butterflies." "None like Mommy, though," Lara laughed, as she backed the car out of the auditorium, and into a sandbox.

Christmas Letter Karma

Oh, I have so much more to tell you about our year and our

life, but the ward nurse has given me the ten-minute warning, so there's just a little time left before they give us our medication and roll us back to our rooms for the night. I wanted to tell you about the trip Sue and I took down to San Diego to see Cecilia Bartoli. Wow! It was like we were both having affairs, but with each other. And about the moth balls in my underwear drawer. Sue bought this very expensive cashmere sweater and to protect it from the moth colony that lives with us, she filled all our drawers with six or seven mothballs. Now when I'm in meetings, people always seem to be sniffing in the air and then looking suspiciously at me and saying things like, "I think we're done here." And about the day we went to the taping of the new T.V. sitcom, Joey, starring Matt LeBlanc. And about Lara's first rock concert, and her first Winter Formal where she walked down the stairway in this glamorous turquoise formal gown and how I looked up and at her and wept and then made a note to myself to call the convent. And there's just so much more.

But the nurse is here now, with the little white cup that contains my pills. She always stands there with this eerie grin on her face and watches to make sure I swallow. They're nice here at the Christmas Letter Rehabilitation Center, but it's not easy trying to kick this Christmas Letter addiction. There are some people here in re-hab who have been writing the same Christmas Letter for the last ten years, just can't seem to catch up with all the things that have happened in their lives that are worth sharing. Actually, the doctors say my case is mild and if I am able to keep this epistle to fewer than fifty pages, they may let me have a home visit for New Years.

So, I have to finish now, but I just can't get those three

wise men out of my mind, not the ones who brought the gifts to baby Jesus on Christmas Eve, but the ones who had to pack up the next day and go back home to the "real" world after having witnessed the greatest miracle and experienced first-hand the greatest promise God has ever made. I mean, don't you think we have a lot in common with those guys? Christmas is over (I'm a little embarrassed to say it's the twenty-sixth), we experienced the miracle of sharing Christmas dinner with Uncle Frank without throwing a turkey leg in rage through the sliding glass door. The gifts have all been opened and many have more than likely already been returned. Jesus was born, and now it's time to get the goats out and clean up the manger. Without any football to watch or the Kobe-Shaq thing to talk about, what were those wise men saying to one another on their long journey home? "Pretty awesome, huh?" "Really. I mean the Savior." "Yeah. In a manger." "Who would have thought?" "What do you think we're supposed to do now?" "I don't know. Let's wait til he grows up and see what he says." "Yeah. But we kind of know what he's going to say. He's going to tell us he's the son of God." "Yeah, well duh. We know THAT." "Yeah. We know that." "Yeah, but what do we do?" "Be good, I guess. He'll want us to be good, right?" "Yeah. I'm going to be VERY good from now on." "Me, too." "Last night was a promise that things here on earth had changed and life for humans was going to be greatly improved." "You think?" "For sure." "It was a promise of everlasting life, which is BIG." "Yeah, everlasting life, at least for most of us." "But so, what do we do? Just go home and wait?" "No. No. You don't get it." "Yeah, well Mr. Third Wise Man, what don't

I get?" "It's a promise made by God, but one that you, we, have to fulfill ourselves." "I knew it! A trick promise, then." "It's a little tricky, yeah." "So, what do you think is going to happen?" "I know what's going to happen." "You can be very pompous sometimes." "But I know. I just know what's going to happen. That's why they call me a Wise Man, for Christ's sake." "So OK, what's going to happen?" "You really want to know?" "Yeah. We want to know." "Yeah. Let us know." "OK. Mankind is going to spend the next 2000 years waiting for Jesus, and all that time, Jesus is going to be waiting for mankind." "You think?" "I'm certain." "Yeah? Well that doesn't sound very smart." "Yeah, well, it's up to us." "Yeah. I guess. It was a great night though, don't you think?" "Yeah. One for the history books." "Hey, by the way, who do you think's going to win the Super Bowl?" "Ha! You don't have to be a wise man for that: have you seen that Tom Brady? He's a keeper. New England, of course."

OK. So from now on, we're going to stop waiting for Jesus, and do something. That's what our family is going to do this year, just as soon as I'm released. We're going to stop waiting around and just be perfect so that Jesus won't have to wait any more, either. I mean what ARE we waiting for? That's what we've decided to do, fulfill the promise, just as soon as we get all those shampoo bottles out of the shower, and get Lara into a good college. I mean you can't even walk around in there without tripping over a plastic bottle. Wait, Where's Lara. That would be a good chore for her. "Lara. Lara. Where are you? Lara!" "I'm up here in the office, Dad; doing Baroque."

Till next year then, our multi-cellular family sends warm

MARK MENDIZZA

wishes to yours. We bid you a belated Merry Christmas and a New Year worthy of the good Lord herself. And please, stop putting it off:

> Be ye therefore perfect, even as your
> Father which is in heaven is perfect.
> Matthew 5:48

With great affection,

Mark, Sue, Lara & PENNY

2003 / 2004
Important Events

- **Open only to students from Harvard, Facebook is launched in February.**
  Dad buys stock in Myspace, as Lara deletes it from computer.

- **Boston Red Sox win World Series for the first time since 1918.**
  "World . . . What?," asks Lara.

- **Space ships, *Spirit* and *Opportunity* land on Mars.**
  Family lands at Mammoth Lakes . . . for vacation.

- **California Governor Gray Davis recalled; Replaced by Arnold Schwarzenegger.**
  Lara once again revises downward her idea of "grown-ups."

- **Space shuttle Columbia explodes, killing all 7 astronauts.**
  Never would have happened in the nineties.

- **CIA admits Iraq posed no imminent threat. C. Powell resigns. GW reelected.**
  Lara wonders why they put Martha Stewart in jail?

- **US transfers sovereignty of Iraq back to the Iraqi people.**
  Sue transfers sovereignty of garage and front lawn to Mark.

2005

The Year of "I'm so Happy!"

Mark, Sue & Lara Mendizza
Orange County, California

December 21, 2005

Dear Friends,

Diing, Ding, Dg! The Christmas bells of 2005 are ringing and oh what a glorious sound they bring, hearkening a new holiday season full of the warmth and good cheer that can only come from 50,000 kilowatts of multi-colored electric lights strung from the eaves and rooftops of all the houses in all the neighborhoods across the land. Ding! Ding! The silver bells are ringing, and yet, most curiously, one never seems to hear a corresponding Dong. Just Dings. Ever notice that with silver bells? From the recorded silver dings inside the mall, to Santa's little dings outside, at the entrance to Nordstrom's, to the ceaseless riff of dings that enter one's head the day after Thanksgiving and remain until a nice cold pitcher of martinis on the first finally releases that much welcome DONG. Till then it's only Dings, which to me is just one more amazing thing about the miracle of Christmas: the complete and total absence of dongs.

This year, however, the heartfelt peal seems to contain the

ring or ding or perhaps even dong of an ending. As the echoing tones drift upward into the brisk (75° F) Southern California air, a kind of Christmas closure is felt, like the sigh at the turning of the final page of a favorite book, or the distant patter of someone running down the street with your purse. Yes, there is something different and disturbing about Christmas 2005 and it calls out for a new title to our Christmas Letter, something that reflects the passing of the era we're wistfully, almost unknowingly, leaving behind. Let's see: ***Christmas 2005, The End of Days***. No. Too Old Testament. ***Christmas 2005, The Year of Living Endlessly.*** No. Too existential. OK: Here it is: ***Christmas 2005, The End.***

Yes. That's it. Clear and succinct. It's over. The sixteen-year saga of Lara Louise Mendizza, so thoroughly documented in Christmas letters from 1988 to 2004, has this Christmas come to a heartfelt and melancholy conclusion. It's over. Childhood. Innocence. Sanity. Lara turned sixteen on November 21st. She got her driver's license on December 2nd. And on the third she drove off into the sunset to meet her girlfriends at the Golden Spoon where, over peppermint and just-chocolate chocolate yogurt, they figured out ways to obtain food, outfits and accessories without ever again having to see or talk to a parent. And so. what's to write in a Christmas letter? It's over.

OK. I have to say I love this group of girls, even though they have evolved from adorable first grade classmates into a savvy, eye-rolling high school posse, entourage, and sometimes girl-gang, depending on the activity and venue de jour. Friday night football game: posse. Winter formal: entourage. "Greenday" Concert: girl-gang. Amanda, Kelly, Deena, Kelsey, Ali, Taylor, Bailey, Lisa and Lara. They call themselves "Ocho" or "El

Ocho" or "Ocho Diablo." Friends since their aspiring parents forced them into advanced, fast-track GATE classes in the third grade; each girl beautiful; each unique, but each sharing a rich common history that has recently given rise to the celebrated, prime time, dramatic masterpiece entitled: *O.C.* Yes. It hurts to admit this publicly, but this is Christmas and we are in O.C. after all, and so we need to ask ourselves: WWJD? Tell the truth, right? They're *OC* girls. They watch *O.C.*. They identify with the characters on *O.C.*. And when it was preempted by an important speech on national defense by the President of the United States, these girls, all of whom are taking advanced physics, calculus and a course on Immanuel Kant, called the station and threatened to boycott not just *O.C.*, but a program called Laguna Beach, one called *One Tree Hill* and one called *America's Next Great Garage Mechanic*. The station, so intimidated by the ferocity of indignant Ocho Diablo, moved the Bush speech to Saturday morning, "with the cartoons, where he belongs," I heard one of the progressive posse members say.

Together these girls see a lot more in T.V., movies and mass media than we do. And I mean that literally. A lot of times I'll be thinking I know SO much more than Lara does just because I was in the French Foreign Legion for a few years, shared peppermint schnapps with the infamous Billy Martin and in a dream, won a Nobel Prize. But then I'll ask her something like, do you think birds were the first creatures to invent the rock and roll song? And I'll get this awesome, insightful answer like, "Birds! Dad! Don't talk to me about birds! And please, whenever any of my friends are around, please don't say ANYTHING. Nothing, OK? Especially about birds!"

I mean these kids see to the depths, the existential, psychological depths of things. Like *O.C.*, for example. They see deeper into the program and its production values than it is possible for a non-teenager who does not suffer from teen brain disease to see. For example, when they watch one of the female characters take her boyfriend's gun and shoot the abusive dude who is rudely strangling her boyfriend with an Armani telephone cord, they don't see a homicide (turned out the boyfriend survived as the girls all knew he would, and the abusive dude later apologized and as punishment was exiled from *O.C.* to Riverside; they don't see a tragedy or even the melodrama of first love, they see ... an outfit, a conspicuously inconspicuous accessory, a poetic riff in the music so artfully choreographed with a camera movement that each girl sighs with the segue and fade to black. When they get together on Thursday night with their popcorn and Jambala Juice, these girls, these Ocho Bonita, don't just see kitsch on *O.C.* (though they see that, too); they see Hamlet at Monarch Bay, *Love's Labor Lost* at the Newport Coast Housing Development. *Twelfth Night* in HD at the Ritz Carlton Hotel.

But this year they shared something else, more relevant to their lives than even the breakup of Maggie and Brent, which was "big." In addition to their transformation from girlhood into young lady-hood, the mystique of a prime time soap opera devoted exclusively to the glossy soul of ***O.C.***, and yet another undefeated MVHS football season, the girls also shared the ancient coming-of-age ritual known in Greek mythology as the CDL, the California Driver's License. Aside from Robert Armstrong (lead singer of "Greenday"), this was the thing they had been dreaming about all year, the day they could drive away on their own, preferably in their own car, with a visa card from Banque Le Dad. Early in the year I remember picking Lara up from school and trying to start up a conversation, which is not easy when you figure that my mind, as a mature, seasoned adult, is concerned mostly with the higher things like finding the Higgs particle, reconciling the Sunnis / Shiite misunderstanding in Iraq and of course trying to remember the recipe for the tortilla soup Sue asked me to make (List on kitchen counter at home). Lara, on the other hand, is more often concerned with, well . . . mascara.

"How'd it go honey?" "Good." "Anything happen at school?" "Not much. How about you?" "Well, you'll be pleased to know I won the Nobel Prize." "Cool," she said, as she placed a "Greenday" CD into the player. "Yeah," I responded. "Not too many people win it twice." She pumped up "Greenday" to a decibel level that cracks the sidewalk. Then she said, "Oh yeah! I forgot, Lisa passed her test. She DROVE to school. Her parents bought her a new Bentley. I mean her parents are SO cool. God I can't wait til I can drive! I wonder what color my car should be. Of course, most of the good colors are taken by now. EVERY-BODY has their license except me." And I'm going, like, right, "Cilantro! Remind me not to forget the cilantro, OK?"

Since making the mistake of placing Lara into advanced Kindergarten before she had teeth, she has always been the youngest member of her peer group, and consequently always the one playing catch up with her older classmates. They had more experienced parents who knew that if they held their kids back and placed them in school later rather than earlier then they would have the advantage not only of being the oldest, biggest and smartest kid in the class, but also the only one with a beard. Plus they would get their learner's permit a whole year before poor Lara would get hers. And that's exactly what happened. Each month another friend passed the driving test and arrived at school the following day in a brand new shiny Bentley (at least that's what Lara told us.) First Lisa. Then Bailey. Then Amanda. Then Kelly. While one posse member after another was being freed from the humiliation of the neighborhood car pool, Lara was still forced to pull up in front of the school with a parent in the car, sometimes even me. Once the kids scooted out, removed their backpacks from the trunk and began walking to class, I would always honk my horn a couple of times and wave enthusiastically to Lara, bidding her much love and a good day of enrichment at school. She would always turn, pull the hood of her sweatshirt over her head and cringe with that adorable look of loathing that comes over her whenever I'm within twenty feet or so. I'd switch the radio station from Brian Seacrest's mammary-based banter to NPR, and drive off waving, with the warm feeling that a parent always gets when they know they've done well by their child.

But all that fun ended on December 2nd. The night before, an unusual thing happened. It was rather late. I was in the den reading *King Lear* and watching the Ali / Frazier fight, which is on every night now on the Joe Frazier Channel. Sue and Lara had gone to a meeting at the school about a Spanish language immersion program in which students go to Spain during the summer, visit Madrid, Sevilla, Cordoba and the Cote de Oro; swim in the warm waters of the Mediterranean, learn more than they should about the boys of Espana and then come home with the amazing ability to say "I didn't know it was due!" in Spanish. The girls had come back late from the meeting and as I read about the mad king who had been so brutally betrayed by his daughters I heard them upstairs rumbling around as they got ready for bed. Then things went silent. Just when I got to the part where Gloucester's eyes were plucked out by evil Cornwall (who was still angry about his name) the door squeaked open and there was Lara in her pajamas. "Hi honey," I said. She said, "I get my license tomorrow. I am just so excited I can't stand it. It's going to be so much fun." This was my Lara. Lovely in her uncensored enthusiasm and glowing with the vague inner vision of an adventurous future free of parents. Lately it had seemed that she had sort of withdrawn from me, which, when you look at me, makes good sense. And I guess it's normal for kids as they grow up and gradually morph into independent people to create a distance between themselves and the authority that parents and adults in general represent. It's sad for us, though. It always feels like something's wrong, but it's not. It's just the way life evolves. But this night Lara was so filled with excitement that she couldn't hold it in. She wanted to share and I was happy about it. It was kind of like the old days when I could tell what was going on with her just by looking and listening with care, instead of sneaking into her backpack and reading the old notes she had forgotten to eat. "It's going to change your life," I said. "A car to a kid is like wings to a bird. You'll be able to fly now." "I know. I just hope I pass." "You're a good driver, Lara. You're an excellent driver. Just go through your checklist of things you have to do. Put it in park. Adjust your seat. Check your mirrors. Hide the beer. Always look behind you when you're backing up." "I just can't wait," she said. "I love you, honey. You'll pass." "I love you, too, Daddy."

At six o'clock the next morning the house shook with the powerful bass riff of *Jimmy Eats World* and plaster fell down onto our expensive fake-down comforter we had made from fake ducks that are raised in Sweden. Lara had hooked her iPod up to the Bose® speakers we bought her last year, and she uses the powerful sound system as an alarm clock. When the house shakes and my ears start bleeding I know it's time to get up. Sue and Lara got dressed and had a quick breakfast. Then they drove off to the San Clemente office of the California Department of Motor Vehicles to take the driving test. I stayed home to work; popped my first brewski of the morning and then slipped into my seat at the high-tech central control center in the office. While working on an ad campaign to help sell gravel, the phone suddenly rang. I looked at caller I.D. and immediately knew it was Sue. Oh my god. What did she want so soon? Did Lara pass? Did she fail? She couldn't have failed. Lara is just too good. She never fails. She auditions for plays and gets parts. In junior high she auditioned to get into and exclusive Film and TV school and she got in. Then she auditioned to switch to musical theater, and she got in. She's stage-managed big shows at the Laguna Playhouse. She stepped up and ran for Secretary of her Junior Class this year and won. She advanced to the Varsity tennis team where she not only lettered in the sport, not only qualified as a "scholar athlete," but also learned how to lose with class. She's smart, and poised. She's lovely and funny. And oh how delicate in her sensibilities and discriminating in taste. I'm serious. She just popped a bag of popcorn in the microwave and instead of just reaching in and taking out a handful like I might do, she inspects each piece individually, literally examines each kernel and nibbles on the inferior corn first, saving the "good ones" to savor at the end. It's a complex process of discriminating observation, evaluation and choice that she brings not just to her popcorn, but to her music, her clothing and even the thoughts she allows herself to have (only the good ones). And then there's her compassion. It's vast. It extends not just to all living creatures except of course her parents and those people within the Republican Party, but even to the inanimate objects of the world. Like her cell phone, for example. To Lara it has feelings just like you and me and they must be honored. For her birthday Mommy gave her one of those cool cell phones on which one can not only watch full-length motion pictures, but actually produce them (the new movie *King Kong* was shot with a cell phone). And you know what? Lara hasn't activated the new phone because she knows it would cause her current phone to feel bad. "I've had this phone for years," she said. "We've just been through too much together for me to deactivate it."

As the phone continues to ring, I feel this surge of outrage. I mean it's always the sweet and innocent who get hurt. Always the sensitive and compassionate ones who are ruthlessly brutalized by the crude, numbing cogs of an inhuman system like the DMV. How cruel. How unjust. How could this be happening? That someone as sweet and kind and deserving as Lara could be failing her damn driving test, and so early in the morning. I finished my Heffeweizen and answered the phone. "This is Mark."

"Honey. Oh, honey!" Sue said. And I thought, oh god, oh god, and reached for the pitcher of margaritas I had had the good sense to place on my file cabinet before sitting down to control central. "Oh honey," Sue repeated. "What? What happened sweetheart. Where are you?" I said. "I'm at the DMV," she whispered, as if doing surveillance. "Well, what happened. Did she pass? She failed, didn't she? I knew it. She was so excited and she failed! Goddamn it! It's just SO unfair. I'm calling the governor. Tell me. Tell me what happened." There was a long pause during which my heart sank and after which Sue, with a trembling, whispering voice said, "She forgot to put it in park!"

Another long pause, just long enough for me to salt the rim of the glass. "Well, does that mean she flunked?" I inquired searchingly. "No, No" she whispered. Why, I wondered, was she whispering? "She hasn't taken her test yet."

And I'm going like what? "She hasn't even taken her test yet?" "No, but when the examiner walked up to the car, Lara just turned it off without putting it in park. She just turned off the car and it was still in drive. I kept nodding and whispering to her, but, " . . . oh honey," she concluded.

Sue was overwrought. The stress not just of the driving test, but of living the last sixteen years with me had been too much. For me, however, this was good. This was a good lesson for all of us. After all, life really IS good. And fair. I mean it's as fair as it can be I guess, without a good lawyer on retainer. And things are never as bad as you think they are. Because if they were . . . nobody would even care if they got a driver's license.

"You mean you called me to tell me she didn't put the car in park, even though she hasn't taken her test yet?" "I was so worried," Sue said. "The guy was right there at the window and I'm sure he saw that she hadn't placed the car in park." "Honey," I said with a depth of understanding and compassion not known since biblical times, "I think we're getting a little ahead of ourselves. Let her take the test and then call me back." "OK," she whispered.

A few minutes later the phone rang again. I knew it was them, but when I picked up the phone I pretended like I didn't. I pretended like it was just another business call. "This is Mark." "Hi Dad." There was a long pause, just long enough to fix the lime to the rim of the glass. "Well,?" I said. "I passed," she responded, only barely containing her effervescent, adolescent glee. "Oh, honey, you're free at last, free at last." "I'm so happy," she replied. "I'm so happy."

It is almost beyond reason or comprehension how relieved and truly grateful those two words – OK, three — can make a father feel, not linked in any way whatsoever to the merits or the cause (a driver's license, a new friend, a good serve, praise, laughter, love, or tickets to "Coldplay"); it doesn't matter. "I'm happy." I think it's the only thing that I truly desire in life anymore: that she find the road that leads to those two, no three, simple words.

Lara passed her test and the next day Sue stood alone on the front porch, like a classic heroine in one of those melodramatic silent movies, and watched her only child drive off into the western sunset, on the way to meet De la Ocho Bonita Diablo at the Golden Spoon. For Sue it was tragic, like the day our little girl walked through the doors and disappeared into the dark cavernous unknown of her kindergarten classroom. It was one of the most memorable and saddest days of Sue's life. She wept then and she wept again when she watched Lara drive down the street by herself for the very first time. I wept, too, because it suddenly dawned on me that she had driven off in my car. With "Greenday" playing so loud one's eyes began to bleed (but in a good way), Lara drove off to meet her destiny, somewhere around the 405 freeway and Laguna Canyon Road. It was over. The End. She's all grown up now, or at least she thinks she is. And so it's over. I mean once the children drive off in your car to meet their destiny, what's left to write about in a Christmas Letter?

The Back Nine

Earlier in the year, before our little family had reached this fateful point, we did take a few trips together. In Spring, the three of us went to Palm Springs. We stayed at La Quinta, which is a resort known for its high-end tennis and even more for the splendor of its several golf courses. Silvester Stallone, having heard that Sue, Lara and I would be staying there, checked in the same day. When we weren't trying to avoid Stallone and his entourage, who wouldn't rest until they had cornered us and asked us all those tedious questions about our personal lives, like how did we get to be so beautiful, what do we eat for breakfast, where did Lara get the backhand; when we weren't avoiding the damned celebrities, we took walks, played tennis and golf . . . er no, we didn't play tennis because Lara is the only one who is good enough to play tennis at LaQuinta and she didn't get up until, like two. But we just hung out and enjoyed being together, at least when Stallone wasn't bugging the shit out us.

While Sue and Lara were sleeping, I would rise early and run up into the stark desert hills overlooking the grounds. It is not surprising that monotheism (Judaism, Christianity and Islam) were all born of the desert. Forests spawn religions with lots of little pagan gods, plus sprites and elves and fairies, not to mention lumberjacks. The desert gives rise to the one singular vision of the sun and the stoicism that comes from an arid land. It was warm while I was running, but the air was still cool and fragrant and the breeze full of whispered messages from that single divine source, hinting at ultimate things, absolute things, the big questions, like can god make hair?

I climbed the hills and once at the top I could almost see the curvature of the earth. I sat there for a while, looking over the vast gray expanse of the desert plane and feeling the subtle sensations of warm floral air, the hard texture of the ground beneath me and the infinity of sky above. This is religious, I thought to myself. If someone didn't know anything about god and was up here like this, I bet they'd just make something up on the spot, probably a monotheism, like "OK, there is totally only one god and if I ever hope to par any of those holes down there, I better start worshipping her right now."

While sitting there entranced by my own deep thoughts, I saw a few monarch-like butterflies flittering about the crags. I turned to look more carefully and instead of a few I saw maybe a hundred. They were flapping their orange-gold wings, but were also surfing the wind to help move them along. Then the hundred became thousands and the thousands became hundreds of thousands and soon the entire hill I was on was shimmering with wave after wave of these beautiful butterflies making their way west . . . or was it east . . . or maybe in a northwesterly direction. For what seemed like hours they migrated past my spot on the mountain, making it pretty clear that something special was taking place. God was sending me a message. And how cool is this, I thought to myself, running back down the hill to tell Sue and Lara all about it.

When I got back to La Quinta the girls were in the restaurant having breakfast. As usual, Lara was explaining in her quiet compassionate way just exactly why she hated us. Sue was finding the ray of sunshine in everything she encountered, which at that moment was a large plate of eggs benedict. Stallone as usual was eaves dropping from the next table. I rushed up and told them about my epiphany, the sun, the desert the butterflies. "It was definitely a sign," I told them. "From the one and only god. If we're ever going to play the back nine of LaQuinta, today is the day we should do it."

Remember, we're not good golfers. Sue and I took some lessons. Lara is a natural. But we hardly ever play and when we do we hardly ever hit the ball. We just love driving the golf cart around in that natural beauty. And the back nine of LaQuinta is legendary for its beauty. I mean there are books, big thick books that catalog the best "holes" in all the world. Not the best courses, but the best holes. And LaQuinta has a couple of them on the back nine because it's just so hard to get the ball in the hole and it's just so gorgeous. To think of Me and Sue and Lara heading to the back nine of LaQuinta in our little golf cart, with the intent to actually golf it, would be like the three of us heading to the Garden of Eden with the intent to barbeque. But over the years we find that we care less and less about how bad we are at things, and just go ahead and do them anyway. Like dancing. Sue and I dance together now, too. She's wonderful of course. Did you know that Sue used to teach dance at Arthur Murray's in Ohio? They still talk about it at the studio in Toledo. But I never learned to dance. I mean you need to know steps and I was always too much of an anarchist to learn any steps, too conforming, too much authority in a "step." And when I tried to dance without steps, paramedics would always arrive and administer some kind of emergency medication. But I took lessons and even though I'm bad and cause other dancers to take up cooking, I can twirl Sue around and we can dance. And sing. I sing now, too, by the way. Even though I can't sing that well, either. Each Thanksgiving, which is also our anniversary, I learn a love song and sing it to Sue live, acapella, in front of dinner guests. So even though we're not that good, we sing. We dance. We play golf. And on that day, me, Lara and Sue, played the back nine of LaQuinta.

Before we could tee off, however, Sue had to change her clothes. True story. We walked up to sign in and the LaQuinta guy behind the counter said, "Madame, we do require a collared shirt on the course." I had a collar. Lara had a collar. But poor Sue, who is of course, by far, the most sartorial and proper of the three, had ventured out that day wearing a little t- with no collar. So we had to go back to the room and help her don appropriate attire for the back nine. Then we got our clubs and cart, and that's when the fun began. Lara of course was the driver, as she always is (more true today than ever). And she was passing cart after cart on the front nine, as we broke LaQuinta speed records making our way to the back.

Did we par? No. Did we bogie? Not really. Did we have a blast? Absolutely. The back nine was a case of reality outrunning apprehension. Every fairway and green was corralled by the low sculpted hills of the high desert, wild flowers were blooming everywhere and, in the stillness, the mystical winds of the one and only god were whispering their messages to us: Grow. Breathe! Keep your head down.

Seeing the way Lara was driving and the way Sue and I were swinging our clubs, all the other golfers chose to flee the back nine. So we pretty much had the whole place to ourselves. And it was paradise. While looking for our balls in the beauty of the surrounding wilderness, we talked about Lara's political campaign. For some reason that is still somewhat of a mystery to us. She decided to run for an office in the Associated Student Body. She had analyzed the candidates and figured she had a shot at winning the office of Secretary of the Junior Class. So, she jumped into the race.

There was only one other candidate for that office, but she was a cheerleader, which gave her a definite advantage. We all know that it was their cheerleading experience in high school that launched the political careers of Condoleeza Rice and Hillary Clinton. So, Lara would have to campaign hard. She designed her own posters and worked with Corinne, one of our graphic artist friends, to create the artwork. All the time we were at La Quinta, we e-mailed proofs back and forth until we got just what Lara wanted. She also worked on the speech she would have to give when she got back. She stayed in touch with all of her friends back home, to make sure she was up to date on the latest polls, which were basically taken at lunch. And three weeks later, she won the election.

But wait, do you see that? What is that walking across the fourteenth fairway? Is that a dog or is that a . . .? With a gait both springy and menacing at the same time, a sly coyote pranced across the fairway, stopped, turned his head to look at us, grinned, then continued up into the hills where he disappeared in the brush just like all our balls.

The Gala

Later that Spring, the three of us attended the big Gala Fundraiser for the Laguna Playhouse. Lara had gone the last three or four years in a row. Each year she and other kids from the Youth Theater have helped sell raffle tickets (they actually raffle off a small country, like last year some lucky real estate developer from Laguna Beach won Finland), and while helping, the kids get to meet cool members of the talented cadre of artists who have passed at one time or another over the boards of the Playhouse stage. Julie Harris one year. Harrison Ford and Colista Flockhart last year. And Sally Struthers in the Spring. We don't normally attend because it costs a lot. Dinner is a million dollars, not including the pass to the martini towers, which stood a remarkable four stories high. For a table of eight you have to deed over a petroleum resource to the playhouse, so it's a pretty exclusive group. Since I was president of the parent's association, however, Sue and I were invited to attend and help out with the kids. It's a very formal affair, and most of the social elite of South County were invited. The women looked like they'd all come from southern plantations before the war. All the men looked like the waiters

We had to be there early, so we were all dressed and ready to go by about five in the afternoon. It was still very warm, bright and sunny outside. And Sue was right when she said it was going to be a weird night. It began when our friend Chrissy stopped her big blue van in the middle of the street. She was driving by our house just as Sue, Lara and I were making our way to the car. When she looked over and saw us, she slammed on her brakes, throwing her kids out the sunroof and into a tree fifty feet away. She opened the door and grabbed her little digital camera and as she jumped down to the ground said, "I've just got to take a picture of this."

Sue in her beautiful turquoise, bare-shouldered formal gown had already walked out of the dusty cardboard clutter of the garage and down the concrete driveway to the waiting white BMW. Lara followed Sue in a lovely, classic black evening dress, and eventually I too walked out of the shadows and into the bright late afternoon sun, still trying to tuck my starched white shirt into the cumber bund of the rented black tuxedo. What Chrissy had witnessed was a scene as rare in our neighborhood as wearing firearms. Formal wear in the suburbs is not just an unusual sight; it's an altogether alien experience for most people around here, especially when the Mendizzas are in them. Chrissy got the shot, and retrieved her kids from the tree.

We picked up Chelsea who was also in a reliable black evening dress. Then Kevin, who was a tall young man wearing his Dad's gray suit. From there we raced down the hill toward the theater. "Why are we going so fast," Lara asked. "We have time." "Yes, we're on schedule aren't we?" added Mommy. But I knew better. I said, "We have to stop at Nana's." And they said, with some alarm, "Oh, we're late then. We're totally late."

Nana is Sue's Mom. The other day she was over here and while we were discussing the situation in Iraq she suddenly asked, "How old am I?" We cringed. She doesn't want to know. "I'm sixty, right?" she continued, and then went on to address the history of Mesopotamia. Nana is ninety-three but we all said, "Right."

We drive up in front of Park Terrace, the assisted care facility where, according to Nana, she is being defrauded out of her life savings. Nana and three other elders were sitting on a wooden bench under the portico at the entrance to the building. One has to put one's self into the orthopedic shoes of the four seniors who were observing our arrival to appreciate how the scene must have appeared. A white BMW drives up and suddenly all four doors swing open, as if an abduction were about to take place or the arrival of the president of AARP. But instead of bodyguards in black suits and scrotum-shaped male ponytails, Sue graciously exits the car in her turquoise strapless gown, looking like the good witch of the North, followed by Lara and Chelsea in their exquisite black evening wear, Kevin in his father's suit and then me, like the member of the rat pack all the other members tried to avoid.

Judging from the twice-furrowed brows of their strained countenances, I'm sure the women on the bench felt their rice paper grasp of reality slip even further away as they tried to make sense of what was before them; perhaps someone at Park Terrace had died inside and this was the funeral party; Or maybe they themselves had died without knowing it, and this was how the afterlife began, swept up to heaven in a new Beemer with angels in formal gowns and ill-fitted tuxedos; or one can imagine a flashback to their own youth when they too had slipped their taut, lithesome bodies into silver satin gowns and illuminated the dimly lit fantasies of men in the 20s and 30s.

Nana looked at the four of us as we gathered together under the portico, but there was no response. She just looked. The point of the visit was to let her see her loved ones – that would be Sue and Lara — all dressed up for the ball. She had said more than once that she'd never seen me in a suit and that her life would have taken one more step toward completion if one day she would be able to do so. Nana adores seeing Lara, no matter how she is dressed, but to see her in a reliable black evening dress would be like Bernadette beholding the Lady at Lourdes. As we grouped together to show her how good we looked, however, and as she stared at us with what I can only call a blank and bewildered look, we realized that she didn't have a clue about who we were or what we were doing there. But how could she? We were all disguised as respectable people. "Nana, its us," we said.

We drove fast to Laguna Beach. We pulled up to the valet

service at the Montage Hotel, which is the newest of several new resort hotels that are appearing like colonial outposts along the coast. The valet opened the door for us and asked, "Are you here for the wedding?" "No. For the gala," we replied. Once out of the car and moving toward the entrance, a woman approached us and asked again, here for the wedding? No, the gala, we said. We found Amy, who was in charge of organizing the event. She gave us a tour of the hotel and showed the kids to the green room. Sue and I remained in the lobby and watched the guests arrive.

The gowns were various in style, color and glory. All of them were statements, from this gown cost more than your house, to this gown values taste over ostentation, to this one is a total utility piece for galas, to this one's to prove what they say about my breasts. We had fun talking to everyone, and as we did, they ceased being elites to us and became just folks, most of whom have worked hard for their place in the social matrix and who were glad they had assets sufficient to bid on Kazakhstan (this year's prize), as well as help the playhouse. Our old friend Tom Wilson, the supervisor of the 5th District walked in and we were surprised when he remembered us. It had been several years since we worked with Tom to defeat the airport, and before that to stop development of the open space behind our homes. Representative Loretta Sanchez came in quite late, after everyone else had gone into the ballroom and the program had begun. We chatted with Loretta. Sue was acquainted with her from the jail because Sanchez had come to one of the graduation ceremonies that Sue had organized for her prized inmates.

Wait. I must digress. Sue had an amazing at experience

during the inmate ceremony she held this year, and I just have to tell you about it. As you know, she coordinates the relationship between Santa Ana College and the educational programs that are offered to the jail system. Each year several of the inmates receive their high school diploma through instruction delivered by the college. This year, something special occurred. After the general ceremony was over and everyone had received their diplomas, there was one left to be awarded. The inmate was so dangerous, however, that he would never be allowed in the same room with the others, who were often incarcerated for minor drug offences. This guy was a killer.

Sue, Loretta Sanchez and a few other people who were there to help honor the work these men and women had done were escorted by several guards to the maximum security area of the jail. There they encountered a man who was cuffed, shackled and under the martial eye of three seasoned guards, each of whom appeared to have eaten their parents. This inmate was extremely dangerous. He was a skinhead. A racist. An Aryan nation dude; angry, fanatical, muscular, treacherous and tattooed. The man's teacher was meeting him in person for the first time. All instruction that had taken place between them took place from a distance, slipping worksheets under the door, passing them back under the security of several guards. He stood shackled and alone, except for Sue, the teacher and her guests.

When he was awarded his diploma something unexpected occurred. He received the acknowledgement with a grace and gratitude that surprised and touched everyone in the room. "This is the first time I have ever completed anything in my life," he said in his chains. "I've never gotten to the goal line with anything I've tried, til now." He began to weep in front of all those people, this fanatic. This monster. And he thanked everyone for helping him to finish something. When Sue came home and told us the story, it stayed with me for a long time. I remember hearing the Dali Lama say that true compassion made a person more confident. I think that's where a lot of Sue's courage comes from and I wanted you to know that this is the kind of thing she is doing when she's not taking Lara to get her drivers' license, or wondering if I'm going to be able to find my way home from Vons.

I took Loretta into the ballroom and helped find her seat. Lara was working the spotlight for the show. The other kids were working the crowd, selling raffle tickets for Kazakhstan. Sally Struthers was up at the podium delivering a very good speech about her career and life, her only regret being that she has still been unable to locate the Higgs particle. Everyone dined, and while dining everyone made numerous trips to the martini towers. They bought raffle tickets and it was fun to watch these sophisticated, affluent people bend their tickets before placing them inside the bowl. Apparently, they believed bending increase the chances of it being picked. Some of the women went into the rest room and sprayed their tickets with hairspray, and then waited until the last minute to place them in the bowl. Everyone wanted Kazakhstan that night.

During the break, Sue and I were standing in the lobby looking for Lara. The gala crowd rushed out and made their way either to the martini towers, the chocolate fountain or the potty. A young woman about our age, slightly intoxicated, but smartly dressed and in possession of a wicked power of perception, walked up to us, almost breathless with emotion. She

118

had been walking past and just couldn't help staring at Sue in her strapless turquoise gown, could not resist the impulse to approach her, to walk right up to her, look her straight in the eye and say, "You know what: you are the most beautiful woman in this room." There was a long pause. Sue stood there gracefully. I seemed to have become invisible. "No. I mean it," said the savvy socialite. "Of all the women in this room, and there are over two hundred of them, you are the most beautiful." And she was. It's quite remarkable, but no matter what room Sue happens to inhabit, well . . . people just know.

But where was Lara? Earlier in the evening, Amy had requested Lara to handle the spotlight during the presentations. She had acquired a reputation I think for being able to handle things, and Amy knew her well from a show that Lara had stage-managed. After Sally's speech though we had lost track of Lara and were just curious about where she might be. While still standing there in the middle of crowd, Sue lighting up the room like a bouquet of candles and I earnestly trying to get my cumber bund to stay straight, we spotted our daughter. She was walking in from the adjacent room with another person, a middle-aged woman, on her arm. We did a double take because we weren't sure if we were getting it right. But there she was, Lara holding Sally Struthers by her arm and waist, holding her up actually, while Sally laughed and continued to tell her stories about her life. We're talking "All in The Family" here; Archie and Edith Bunker, icons from the seventies. I mean last year she was holding up Harrison Ford who had also scaled the martini towers, and like this year she's holding up Gloria Bunker-Stivic. And she hardly even knows who they are. "Charmed life," I say to Sue. She lives a charmed life. And so do I.

Six months later, Lara was driving down our street alone, on the way to her next charmed experience. And for us, that was "The End," at least of life AND Christmas as we knew it. But you know what? She suddenly stopped. She turned around and headed back to us. Apparently Lara had forgotten her ... mascara. And wait! What about gas? And La Ocho Dinero via Mi Padre, which she had also, in her excitement, forgotten to withdraw from Banque Le Dad. I mean Lara was back before the sad melodramatic scene could regain its foothold, or Sue wipe the tears from her eyes.

Proof once again, don't you think, that there are no real "endings." No "dongs." When one rides (or drives) off into the sunset, what happens? One ventures over the next horizon, into the great unknown where no man or woman has gone before. One slays the dragon, discovers the secret code and wins the hand of one's beloved; then one finds a job selling time shares and gets back to the ecstasy of spectator sports. Only in the movies is there such a thing as The End. In life, nothing ends; it segues, transitions and recycles, but it never ends. I mean aside from fueling the entire U.S. GNP, that's the true meaning of Christmas itself. That there is no end. That life is everlasting. That the Christ is born within us each and every moment.

Well, for us, anyway, that's the meaning. And so this is not the end. It's the beginning. Of the next chapter in Lara's charmed and forever charming life, of Sue's inextinguishable light and my quest for a more perfect cumber bund. It may be the last Christmas Letter we write, but it's the first page of an entirely new era for us and the world. Our Christmas wish this year is that your new beginnings be filled with the irrational exuberance of your one and only god, and that you find the road that leads to "I'm so Happy."

We'll meet you there,
With love,

Mark, Sue, Lara and Penny

Dong!

2005
Important Events

- **Ellen Johnson Sirleaf becomes first female president of African country (Liberia).**
  Lara runs for Secretary of Junior Class, and wins.

- **Tom Brady leads New England Patriots to Super Bowl for third time.**
  Lara wins third place singles in Saddleback District Tennis Tournament.

- **Last year it was Facebook. This year YouTube was launched.**
  Exhausted by real life, nation switches attention to kittens.

- **The Disneyland Resort celebrates 50th birthday.**
  Daddy tells Lara he was first person on Dumbo ride.

- **Rosa Parks dies at 92. First woman to lie in the United States Capitol rotunda.**
  Lara awakening at 16. Stands up for self and others.

- **Hurricane Katrina devastates Gulf Coasts.**
  Prince Charles marries Camilla Parker Bowles.

- **Lara gets driver's license.**
  Drives off forever . . . in our car.

2006

The Year of the
Winter Formal

Mark, Sue & Lara Mendizza
Orange County, California

December, 2006

Dear Friends, Relatives and Others;

Usually in our Christmas letter we try to cover all the cool things that have happened during the year in Southern California, like fires, earthquakes, celebrity break ups and when California elects a governor who can actually pronounce the word "California" without sounding like a cartoon character: "KALIFORN-EEYA." After that, as most of you know, I launch into an endearing and seemingly endless account of our lives with the kids. This year, however, two things prevent me from doing this: first, none of those things happened in Southern California this year and second, Sue says we don't have kids. She says we have a dog: Penny. And we have a website on MySpace we're very fond off, but no kids. Which was a big surprise to me.

I know what you're thinking. What about Lara? For seventeen years the Christmas Letter has been about Lara: her first poopie in the potty (which people are still talking about), her first words ("I need twenty dollars"); and things like remember back in 1998 when we spent the entire year trying to find her shoes? I mean that was worth a chapter. But, alas: once kids turn seventeen like Lara did this year, or sixteen, or these days maybe even four, they're not exactly kids anymore; they're more like ... roommates who won't clean up and who don't really like you very much. It's a hard transition to make, but let me assure you: What you lose in innocence and affection, you more than make up for in emotional "drama" and credit card debt.

Which is fine I guess. Which is life. Which is God's way of paying you back for when you undid your own parent's mental health. But it doesn't work that well at Christmas time, when you're sitting before the crackling fire (that just erupted on the hillside outside of your window, by the way) sipping a whisky 'n' nog and pining nostalgically over Christmas past, when our dear Lara shimmered like tinsel on the tree in anticipation of Christmas morning. Those were the days! When a little green ball or a Curious George book would fulfill Lara's every dream; at least for a few minutes.

This year, it's going to take a little more than that, like probably the condo she's had her eye on. She still glows, of course. She'll always glow, but I think it's due more to this new high-tek soft drink they call "VAULT," than looking forward to opening the gifts under the tree. It's more like a radioactive, adolescent glow in anticipation of the trip she and her friends are going to take up to the mountains, where I believe they plan to do some of the things they witnessed in the movie Saw VI. I jest, of course, and am reminded of something I read recently by the great poet and engraver William Blake,

> He who binds himself to a joy
> Does the winged life destroy.
> But he who kisses the joy as it flies
> Lives in eternity's sunrise.
>   Wm. Blake

128

I know what you're thinking? What about the scrapbook? What about the live-action DVDs we produce of our kid's soccer, volleyball, football, baseball, basketball, ballet, jazz and modern dance; what about the recitals, birthdays, vacations, and you know what I mean? That sounds more like binding one's joy in the scrapbook than kissing it as it flies by; don't you think?

And guess what. Blake suffered big time for those four lines. The Precious Memories industry of the late 18th century in London sued poor William for what they called poetic degradation of precious memories. This was 1790, you have to remember, a time of revolution and change, especially in the area of scrapbooks. Kissing a joy as it flies instead of thoroughly documenting and storing it in the garage ("binding it" as we say) with hard copies and ticket stubs was considered subversive. People wanted photos of the kids manning the barricades and standing next to the guillotine, and anyone who interfered with that could be prosecuted under the Precious Memories Degradation Act of 1789.

But wait! I know what you're thinking? What the heck is he talking about? This is a Christmas Letter. What about Lara's Winter Formal? Her stay in Washington D.C. last summer? What about the celebrity sightings and the award she received as best two-legged student and the one for being a scholar athlete? And of course, the big question ? Where's Lara going to college next year?

OK: it's true. I've gotten off track. But this digression was planned; it was carefully designed to lead to one of the important things that has happened to the family this year: my ADD diagnosis. Yup! It finally came through. We've been working on getting an ADD certificate for me for several years, and it finally came in. It was the trip to Africa I think that did it. I left the office for a photo shoot at the studio in Newport Beach one morning and ended up two days later working in Zimbabwe as a physician. Definitely ADD, they said, and you know what that means: Excuses! I now have an excuse for everything. It's why I haven't called. It's why I forget your name. It's why this Christmas Letter will have things in it about Easter.

And of course I'm just kidding about our Lara. She remains the light of our lives; we just have to share her with so many other people these days who are also kissing the joys of her radiant presence as they fly by in flocks.

In fact, this year she is providing light for the entire neighborhood. Check this out: Just to show Lara that even though she has abandoned her obligation to provide justification for Mommy's and Daddy's existence, and, without our permission, went ahead and became a uniquely intelligent, beautiful, poised, articulate and popular young woman in her own right, with her own spirit and her own silly ideas, we still love her more than most of our expensive belongings. And just to make sure she knows that, and that her self-esteem has not been negatively affected by the pressures of growing up, which the few of us who have actually done so know can be difficult, we created an over-sized, illuminated and inflatable plastic figure of Lara, and placed it on our roof this Christmas, instead of all those colored lights. Wow! Christmas Lara just lights up the whole street! In fact, she dwarfs the attempts by our neighbors to light up their homes, which still use deer, snowmen and holy families instead of inflatable versions of their own kids, which are fairly inexpensive these days and which we honestly believe Jesus would prefer. I don't know about your neighborhood, but there's a lot of competition for best-lit house around here, and I think our Christmas Lara has taken first prize this year. Every night, she's up there on the roof, blinking on-and-off, a holiday token to our love for her, and taking the phrase "let-your-light-shine" to a whole new level.

At first, I have to say Lara was a little disturbed at our holiday tribute, but since packing up and moving to another country (won't tell us which one), she seems to have, you know, matured into it.

But I know what you're thinking? What about the rest of the year? What did we do in February and March? What about Springtime and Summer? Well, I don't need to tell you it was eventful, and I also don't need to tell you every moment is worthy of being included in this Christmas Letter for 2006. As I have said before, abbreviating one's life in the name of brevity, is like shortening one's life in order to make a train, which, like the rest of this letter, makes no sense whatsoever.

OK: First, just to prove she no longer needs us very much, Lara was named co-captain of Mission Viejo High School Varsity Girls Tennis. This was a very cool honor, because it required a vote of her teammates and coach, and was a reflection of the respect and affection they all had for her. I kept telling them that Lara should learn to become captain of her room first, like to order herself to pick up her clothes and stuff, but that concept seemed to go over everyone's head. They still wanted Lara as their captain, and she led them through the entire season. I was so proud of her.

Winter Formal

And while she was leading the team to their grudge match with Dana High, Lara also had the Winter Formal to deal with. This was an important event in her life because it involved shopping. It held a deep meaning that was actually symbolized by the very name of the event itself. The word "Winter" was cleverly meant to designate the season in which the dance was to be held. And the word "Formal" was a code word meant to designate "Insanely Expensive Dress that Shows Breasts and Will ONLY Be Worn ONCE."

That was the challenge for the three hundred or so young women who were going to participate in this annual coming of age ritual: finding a dress that a) showed breasts, and b) that no one else had already found. It was quite a drama in our house. Both Sue and Lara kept coming home with dresses to try on. After a week of this, they finally nailed it down to a blue one and a red one. The blue was elegant and understated. The red was, as Lara described it, "like Nicole Kidman in the poster I have of Moulin Rouge." It was fiery and flamboyant, and no one could decide which dress was the best.

"I like the red one," I said. "But it totally depends on how you feel, your mood."

"I know," Lara responded. "But I can't decide, even how I feel."

So she took photos of herself in both dresses and uploaded them to MySpace.com. Then she asked all of her friends to vote on which dress she should wear. Alex voted blue. Taylor, red. . . ., etc. Balloting went on for a few days, during which Lara was also supposed to be studying for a big test in history. The dress issue intruded greatly on her study sessions, and fortunately I was there to nag her incessantly. Also, I'm pretty good at history myself, as long as it wasn't too long ago; and between the NFC and AFC championship playoffs I would go up to Lara's room where she was conducting the dress elections and offer to help her out with the chapter on last Tuesday.

In the meantime, Sue had gone over to visit her mother at the assisted-care place that has been helping Nana to stay on her feet while walking. As an only child, Sue is the sole companion and caregiver for her mom, who is well into her ninth decade. She's still bright and alert, and although she's given up competing in Iron Man events, she still participates in those new elder-sports games like competitive standing up and sitting-down. Between Lara's needs as a young scholar-athlete-prom-going-thespian-teenager and her mom's needs as an older person trying to remember where the front door is, Sue really has her hands full, especially since she also has to run most of Santa Ana Community College where she is a full professor in charge of just about everything. Plus. she has to pretend sometimes to actually listen to me while I try to explain how I ended up in Mogadishu working as a U.N. peacekeeper when I was supposed to take the dog to the vet. Poor Sue!

Anyway, after visiting her mother, Sue went to hit a few balls. That's right! I don't know if I mentioned this in last year's Christmas Letter, but Sue and I have taken up golf. We had taken up dancing the year before, but then we found out that dancing takes place mostly at night. That was a problem. Sue has always believed that nighttime was the best time to be in bed. From her point of view, daytime is like for being awake, and night is for like sleeping (go figure!). We searched for a cool Glen Miller swing orchestra and a ballroom that offered lunch-dancing, but alas: Another concept too advanced for the culture. And Sue just didn't want to give up bed for salsa dancing, especially the way I did it.

But then she found out that people mostly play golf during daylight hours when they were mostly conscious, plus it was done outdoors in beautiful surroundings. Well, that was it: we gave up swinging on the dance floor for swinging on the golf course.

And as you probably know, I'm pretty much a natural athlete, which is why I am able to drink a few schooners of beer and still stare numbly at NFL games on the television set for six or seven hours without getting winded. Sue, however, doesn't have that kind of training, and so she did something that to this day I don't really understand: she took lessons. When she began, she looked awkward, like a character from a silent movie. But then, by doing something that seemed unfair to me, she stuck with it. She practiced. And now she looks as cool as Ms. Wu.

"I didn't do too well," she said when she returned to the house where I was betting our home equity on Seattle, and Lara was still upstairs counting dress ballots instead of studying the differences between Madison and Jefferson. "I think I may have hurt my neck." "I told you, you shouldn't practice," I counseled. "You know, those PGA guys won't tell you this, but a person only has so many good strokes inside of them, and if you waste them practicing, then you won't have any left for real golf."

Sue asked if Lara was reading her history. I said I think so. She always says she is, but there's no way of knowing for sure. She sits in front of her computer staring at the screen and whenever we ask what she's doing she always says she's solving differential equations or writing essays on the Elizabethan sonnet. At this age, a parent can only pry so much into the secret lives of their teens, but it seemed to us that if Lara were studying her physics as much as she told us she had then she would for sure receive the Nobel Prize by second semester. The strange thing is that she never says, "I'm on MySpace counting dress votes." Sue went upstairs and gathered together all the dresses that had accumulated in Lara's bedroom, and wrapped them up to take back to the stores, all of them except of course the red one and blue one.

Lara was stunning in her red dress; Dare I say she "glowed." Sue and I and about thirty other pairs of teen-worn parents were down at the artificial lake to take photos of our enviable off-spring, all dressed in elegant formal gowns; luscious young girls in satin reds, chiffon pinks, purples, blacks and blues; and their geeky guys in tuxedos and tennis shoes. Lara was there with all her friends and John, who was her date, a pretty cool guy, considering the intentions that evolution has installed within his gender, and the sordid thoughts that lurked in his mind.

It was like one of those Disney movies that Lara used to watch: all the kids kind of blond and perfect with a high contrast video glow. But to Sue and I it was another strange gathering. For one thing, many of the parents looked like teens themselves, except they were grinding their teeth a lot and carried cameras. They probably seemed young because Sue and I are what is known as OPs (Older Parents), and studies have found that being old makes everyone else seem younger.

It was also strange because everything seems a little strange to me. No matter where I find myself in life, I always feel a little like, "Whoa, how did I get here?" (I'm including Tehran, Iran; Ras Tanura, Saudi Arabia, Beirut, Bucharest, Budapest, the hill tribes above Chaing Mai, Thailand, Managua during the Sandinista rule, and of course Fashion Island in Newport Beach.) It's all a little strange, and I always tend to feel like I'm in a foreign land, listening to natives talk about their lives and culture. Only this time its mine, or ours.

Even Lara surprises me sometimes. Like I walk up to her. She's all fiery red in the Kidman dress and dispersing herself glibly to the crowd of peers; she's wound up in a highly social-mode, joking with John, holding a white rose bud, a boutonnière, in her left hand and her silver purse over her shoulder. Like all the other parents, I approach to take a photograph, to capture (bind) an historical moment in our lives. This feels normal. But then Lara goes, how do I pin this on? She suddenly turns to me and says, Dad pin this on. Huh? This shocks me because she has always been so self-conscious about introducing us to her boyfriends, let alone allowing us close enough to pin a boutonnière on a lapel. But I'm cool. I flow. I hand the camera to Lara and I fiddle with the little pin that has been stuck through the stem of the boutonniere. I take the satin lapel between my fingers and try to figure out the best way to attach the white rose, and all the while John, who I have barely met before, stands there with a remarkable patience and good will. I was cajoled out of the background where, like a good OP, I was sort of concealing myself behind the camera, and into the high definition world of teen-glow.

"You know the dance will be over and we'll still be here trying to get this rose on your lapel," I said to John, wiping the blood from his coat. "You're not a bleeder, are you?"

The Lost City

Springtime for our family was all about standardized tests and celebrities: Advanced Placement Tests, SAT Tests, and Arnold Schwarzenegger. Lara and her friends take mostly AP courses in high school. These are History, English, Math and Science courses that qualify for college credit. But after the class you have to take a standardized test to prove you know the stuff, and obtain a certain score in order to get the college units. The AP tests are in May, and so there's a big push to study for them in April. And then later they have to take those SAT tests. We decided to take Lara and three friends down to Mexico, where they could get away from the temptation of *Gray's Anatomy* and

South Coast Plaza and spend some time at the pool figuring out who came first: Madison or Monroe? Before heading south for the cram session, however, we had to go to this big Hollywood premiere of Andy Garcia's new movie, *The Lost City*.

This was our first Hollywood premiere, and the girls – Sue, Lara and Lara's friend Kelly — were pretty stoked. They didn't know exactly what to expect, but they did know that life would not be the same, that they were about to touch the hem of immortality or at least feast from the same popcorn box as Dustin Hoffman. As a male, however, it was my job to hide my enthusiasm and pretend that the premiere was pretty much routine, like getting my tires rotated. I mean even if Matt Damon likes me and wants to be my best friend, what then? Is he going to let me star in his next movie? Are we going to adopt a baby from Africa together? I don't think so.

But still, I have to admit, deep inside I was secretly looking out for Jennifer Lopez or Angelie Jolie or maybe even Tuesday Weld.

The Arclight is a trippy theater. It's the old Cinerama building on Sunset Boulevard, sort of round and enormous like a Radio City Music Hall that shrunk. Outside there was a red carpet, searchlights and lots of paparazzi. As we approached the crowd that was assembled outside the theater, however, our initial reaction was one of disappointment. We thought maybe we had overdressed (Lara and Kelly were wearing beautiful dresses, and Sue looked like Tuesday Weld.)

"These people don't look like celebrities," I said to Lara, who was already distancing herself from me. "They don't even look as good as we do." And that's because they weren't celebrities. We'd gotten in the wrong line. These people weren't even invited to the premiere. They were there to watch people who were invited, people like us, walk into the theater. Excuse me, I said to one guy who was still wearing his mailman uniform, but can you tell us where the important people go?

We walked around the corner toward the secret entrance for guests, and stopped at the elevator that would take us up to where Dustin Hoffman and Tuesday Weld were waiting to meet us. The doors opened and guess who walked out? Robert DeNiro? Nope. Jennifer Aniston? No again. (btw: would someone please find Jennifer Aniston a husband?) Give up? OK. Bill Murray. He was one of the stars of the movie. He was standing there in the elevator wearing white linen slacks, a Hawaiian shirt and a white linen sport coat. He had a gimlet in his hand, and as he bounded out of the elevator, he saw Lara, Kelly and Sue and was so taken by their beauty that he had to pause and say hi. "Hi," he said. Then he ambled across the street where the party would be held after the screening. We all turned to one another and said, "Was that Bill Murray?"

Once inside the Arclight, it was exactly what we thought a Hollywood premiere might look like. The lobby was alive with hundreds of people wearing black outfits, acting nonchalant and air kissing even when there was no one in front of them. We could see the strobe lights flashing and the paparazzi taking photographs outside as more and more celebrities arrived. There was a mountain of popcorn boxes in the center of the lobby, literally a mountain about twelve feet high, and you just walked up and took a box. There were also those free gift bags that contained all kinds of free products like hand crème, mascara, espresso coffee cups, CDs with music from the *The Lost City,* and of course a gift certificate for a free house. The excitement was definitely there now, and the girls were glad they had worn their good dresses.

Before the movie screened, Andy Garcia walked out on stage

and told the story of how the film had been made. It was a true labor of love, all about his native Havana and how it had been taken away from him and millions of other Cubans by Fidel Castro and a revolution that had degraded into a military dictatorship instead of a genuine liberation. "That happens a lot," I explained to Lara and Kelly.

Garcia had worked on the film, trying to raise the money and get a script with which he could work, for over sixteen years. He got Dustin Hoffman and Bill Murray to join the project and tried to find Tuesday Weld, but apparently no luck there. Garcia called the whole cast to join him down on the stage and even though Bill Murray was in the back row making little fart noises with his hands, tears came to Andy's eyes as he described his beloved Havana. I leaned over to Lara and Kelly and said sagaciously, "We're really lucky to live in a town no one wants to take over."

The movie itself wasn't very good. I think it was the script. It had been written by a Cuban poet named C. Cabrera Infante who was like the Shakespeare of Havana. He was of course an exile from Castro's Cuba and people just loved him. In its original version, the script was something like six hundred pages long – not including poems — and movie time is calculated at about a minute per page. So you can imagine Garcia's challenge. Infante was a great poet, but a bad screenwriter and Garcia loved this guy so much that he didn't have the heart to cut the script down to where it would have been manageable. Just to emphasize the point, it was said that Cabrera's Christmas Letters went like twenty, sometimes even thirty pages long; I mean what kind of vain, disturbed person would do something like that?

After the screening we walked next door to the big Hollywood cast party, and THAT was very cool. There was a full Cuban buffet with food from Cuba, an open Cuban bar, and an excellent Cuban jazz ensemble that was not only very hot, but also totally Cuban. Garcia, I think not only directed the film, but also composed much of the music and we got to chat with him and then watch him play the bongos, which I'd always dreamed of seeing. Sue and I found a safe corner where we could take in the scene, and Lara and Kelly cruised the party. They'd wander back every once in a while, and tell us about the stars they'd touched, and for some reason they kept running into Murray; at the bar, on the little bridge, in the ladies room.

It was about midnight and we were getting ready to go when I saw Murray talking to a small group of people. I said to Lara and Kelly, "Come on: let's go talk to the guy. He's totally approachable." I tried to coax the girls over to where he was standing, but they were very shy. "Please don't," they said nervously as I suavely dragged them by their skirts across the floor, trying frantically to get them closer to the guy who made *Caddyshack* and the unforgettable *Ghostbuster Trilogy,* which in my opinion were superior to anything Godard, Truffaut or Coppola ever did.

"Wait! He's alone. Let's go," I insisted. But the girls were adamant. They thought I was an idiot. It would be such a gross, unseemly intrusion on Murray's privacy, they said, that even with all of my cool sophisticated maneuvers, all the two of them wanted was for me to please die now. Fortunately, I had long ago abandoned any sense of shame or dignity, and with Sue, Lara and Kelly right behind me, I just walked up to Murray and said "Would you mind? My daughter is just dying to meet you."

Bill Murray was really very cordial, and totally willing not just to meet the girls, but to take them back to his place. "Sure," he said. And then paused a moment and looked quizzically behind me. "But, ah, what daughter?"

Huh? When I turned around I saw that all three girls had

gone. And this is where my training as a seasoned jerk really came in handy. "I swear she was here just a second ago. Wait here, OK."

I found the girls hiding behind a large Cuban that had come to United States from Cuba. I gently shoved them back to Bill, who was waiting patiently to speak with Lara, Kelly and Sue. They honestly had a great time; talked about school, Hollywood, Murray's role in *Lost in Translation*, and of course going back to his place. The girls said no, they had to go to Mexico the next day to study for AP exams. So, Bill did a cute little pose for a photo with Lara and Kelly. I of course was the photographer, but guess what? I couldn't get the flash to flash. "Wait," I said coolly. "Wait, OK. OK. OK. OK. I think I have it. OK."

And click. I got the shot. The girls said goodbye to Murray and as they were walking away Bill stopped Lara and said, "You know. You're Dad's a real 'spaz." Lara paused, nodded and replied, "Tell me about it."

Make Way for the Governor

When we got back from the intensive study session in Mexico, Lara and I began working on the little documentary film we had planned to make for KidSingers. That's where we met Arnold Schwarzenegger. Have I told you about KidSingers? It's an inner-city youth chorus made up of about a hundred at-risk kids who are finding support and a pathway to success in music. I sit on the board and as any board member of any non-profit knows, fundraising is not only a perennial, but also a constant need. The best way to raise money for the kids is for more people to see and hear them sing, but it's just very hard to transport a hundred kids around town, especially at-risk kids who have to be transported one at a time, and always with at least two armed guards, one of which must be Cuban. So, Lara thought it would be a good thing to make a movie about the kids. That way more people could see, hear and ultimately pay to send the at-risk child to Stanford University. Lara and I began by shooting rehearsals and concerts. Then we scheduled individual interviews with some of the kids. This was really an enlightening experience for both Lara and me. It was one thing to be with the kids in their costumes at rehearsal where they were all in a group, and something quite different to go to their homes and speak with them about their experience both with KidSingers and life in general.

The filming took us deeper into their lives than even some of the music instructors have been. Evelina is a Latina with a voice like an angel, but her parents don't want her to sing. They discourage or at best ignore her. Brian and Ayeesha are black. They're brother and sister. Their parents are gone and they are being raised by their grandmother who was born and raised in the segregated south. Brian, Ayeesha and their grandmother sing gospels in their house together every Sunday morning. Huver's small apartment is very crowded, but until recently at least his mom and dad were there for him. We found out about a month ago that Huver's father had died of a heart attack, which is going to be extremely hard on the entire family. Katrina had lived with the sound of gunfire every night. Recently she was able to move out of the dangerous neighborhood and into a location that was much safer. All these kids are talented, and they're all pretty brave, too. Lara and I learned a lot from them. The social and cultural differences are big, but what the kids have in common, their music and their sprit, are even bigger. "All we have to do to overcome our differences," said Lara, "is get closer to one another. And maybe sing."

One day we were interviewing Vanessa about her KidSinger experience when we received a call from Paul, the founder of KidSingers. He had received a request for some of the kids to come and sing at a big event where Arnold Schwarzenegger was scheduled to speak. Paul was at the hotel, and he thought it might be cool if we could tape the kids singing for the governor. He said with my prison record he didn't think he could obtain security passes for Lara and me, but maybe we could come over to the hotel with the camera and teach him or Beverly his wife – who is really the mainspring to the choir — how to use it, and they could tape the kids singing from their table.

We finished listening to Vanessa tell us how much the KidSinger program had meant to her, and then we packed up and drove to Newport Beach where the governor was going to speak with Orange County business leaders about tax breaks, and then ask them to give him sixty million dollars for his campaign. Lara and I arrived and found Paul in the lobby where he was asking the same business leaders for like a buck fifty to support the kids. Before giving him the camera, we had to check the lighting in the ballroom, so Paul escorted us down the long corridor, past a ton of security people who were all talking into their lapels. We entered the ballroom, which was big and lavish. Lara set about checking the lighting and setting the white balance on the camera. I asked her if I could help, but she just rolled her eyes up into the top of her head, which is our code for "Seriously, Dad."

Then we started walking back through the kitchen again, heading back to the lobby. But before we reached the swinging kitchen doors we heard this loud, urgent voice behind us. "Make way!" said the voice. "Make way for the Governor!" What the heck? The Governor was apparently walking through the kitchen, too; probably so he didn't have to talk to all those business leaders in the lobby until he learned English. "Make way," came the voice again, and this time the secret service guy wasn't talking into his lapel. All the chefs and prep cooks and busboys parted like the Red Sea. Paul moved to one side, and Lara and I moved to the other side and looked back toward where the deserts were being made. Down the widening corridor came Arnold Schwarzenegger, buffed, bright and rocking a little to the left and right as he walked straight toward us. He is a bigger than life kind of guy, even though he's a lot shorter than you might think. It kind of caught us off guard. I mean I knew this was our year for meeting celebrities, but I didn't know I'd be meeting them in the kitchen.

Arnold walked up to us and almost knocked us over with his charisma. Paul Folino, a major player in Orange County politics, had also snuck into the kitchen so he could give Arnold all his money before any of the other Orange County business leaders could give him all of theirs. Apparently the first one to give him their money gets to feel a bicep. Folino was standing right next to Lara and I and Arnold greeted him jovially, "Look at you in a new pin striped suit," he said, shaking Folino's hand. "Can you believe it, Paul, I'm the governor of Caleeeefornia?"

Then he turned to Lara and me. I have to admit I was a little star struck, but as always I maintained my composure and asked the Governor in a very sophisticated way if he wanted to Indian Wrestle. And then I turned and introduced Lara. "This is my daughter Lara," I said. The Governor turned to Lara and smiled loudly. "Hello," he said. "Did you know I was the governor of Caleeeeefornia?" Lara, always as poised and charming as her father, responded, "It is a pleasure to meet, sire." Then

Schwarzenegger did something a little strange. He glanced at me and then leaned over to Lara and whispered in her ear, "You know your Dad is kind of a ... well sort of a spaz?"

Then he was whisked through the swinging kitchen doors into the ballroom where Orange County's elite business leaders would listen to the KidSingers sing their hearts out, and then give the Governor all their money.

"Tell me about it," Lara said.

OK. Those are just two of the many celebrity encounters we've had this year. The truth is, Lara has been doing better at this that Sue or I; though Sue's not doing bad. While I was getting my hair cut one day this summer, she met Larry King in front of the Beverly Hills Hotel. He just walks by, and like everyone else, couldn't resist staring at my wife while she was sipping her tea and contemplating the consumption of a snow pea from the porcelain plate in front her. "Hi," says Larry as he walks by dazed, trying to interview himself about the experience.

But Lara's definitely done the best. Even after meeting all those powerful people in Washington (which I will tell you about soon), she came home and at the KROQ Almost Acoustic Christmas Concert found herself sitting next to Toby McGuire. And during a field trip to the Los Angeles County Museum of Art with her Humanities class she met the guy who created that show that turned into that movie that turned into that franchise called "Jackass." And then at the La Brea Tar Pits she met this guy from *One Tree Hill*, or *O.C.* or *Laguna Beach*, or *Divorced Women of South Orange County* or one of those shows.

The point is, the closer one gets to celebrities the closer one is to God. And so we as a family are feeling particularly spiritual this year and really giving thanks for all the good fortune we have, not only in terms of the material things like food, good coffee and designer clothes, but also in terms of the higher things like making contact with the guy who did "Jackass."

But I know what you're thinking? What about the summer? What about those powerful people from Washington D.C.?

OK. If last winter was about Winter Formal and last Spring was about standardized tests and celebrities, then last Summer was a lot more serious. Last summer was about nuclear non-proliferation.

Lara and her friend Kelly signed up with an organization called Junior Statesmen of America to spend a month at Georgetown University in Washington D.C. studying U.S. Foreign Policy. No. I'm not kidding.

This was a bold decision for Lara, first of all because it meant that instead of going to the beach during the summer, she'd be writing long, hard papers on national security issues. "Better you than our President," I said when I found out her plans. And second because the kids that go to these things are hardcore. "They wear pocket protectors," Lara complained. "Instead of going to football games on Friday night, they stay home and write editorials."

I don't know what exactly prompted her to take on this challenge, except for the fact that Lara really does like being with smart people, which is why she tends to spend so much time away from the house. Ocho is smart. (Have I told you about Ocho? Ocho is the group of eight girls who have been together since being forced into GATE classes back in third grade. It's Lara's core peer group, and has evolved in strange ways to include a lot of girls and even some guys who weren't charter members. In a way Ocho has morphed over the years into a kind of social institution with rites and rituals all its own, like counting in multiples of eight. Everyone in Ocho is smart.)

And the girls on varsity tennis are smart, too. There are like seven scholar athletes on the team, including Lara, which means they had to attain something like a 3.8 GPA, plus answer the question, who was Gottfried Leibnitz? And I'm telling you, the kids in her Humanities class are totally smart. (Of course, I have to ask the question, what are they doing in a Humanities class in high school in the first place? I mean why aren't they taking typing and auto shop like I did at their age?). Anyway, we just heard that Jared was accepted to Yale. Fucking Yale! Ricky was accepted at Harvard. And Marie was accepted at Stanford. All these kids are in Lara's Humanities class. So I guess it was just the idea of being 3000 miles away from me, living in the dorms at Georgetown and hanging out with kids that know how GPS works that attracted her. Sue and I, on the other hand, felt it would be a good place for Lara to learn some hard life lessons: like how to get up and make her bed on her own. But I didn't just let her fly off without letting her know what she was getting into. I counseled her. I said, "You know Washington D. C. is Hollywood for ugly people, don't you?"

To be honest, we were a little worried. Lara had never been away on her own for a month before. I mean mentally she was always living in some kind of a foreign land, but geographically she had never gone away for that long. And I hate to say it, but by the beginning of her second day, our worst fears were realized. We got the message on our answering machine, "Hi Mom. Hi Dad. This is Lara. We got here okay, but it's hot, there's no food, and . . . we just want to come home."

By the end of the second day, however, a strange transformation began to take place. Lara made friends. They formed a posse, something like an East coast Ocho. Yes: the kids were hardcore brilliant, but they were also remarkably imaginative, committed and kind. Rachel was beautiful, with a spirit that lit up the dorm like the Washington Monument. Danny was so smart, Condolezza Rice actually let him run U.S. foreign policy for two weeks while she tried to explain the concept of "vocabulary" to President Bush. And Liza was mad! It was perfect. We never heard from Lara again.

Instead of the beach, she visited "the hill' in the morning, attended lectures in the afternoon and debated every night. She met Diane Feinstein, Karen Hughes, tons of other senators, congress people and the Israeli and Palestinian ambassadors. She had lunch at the French Embassy, which in her words "was very disappointing." She really got a sense of how Washington worked, but mostly she had a blast with these kids from all over the country.

Lara had performed under pressure before: on stage, on the tennis court and in some of those intense shopping situations, but standing in a hall before hundreds of people whom she had grown to really admire, and arguing her position on nuclear non-proliferation was new ground for her. There was no time to prepare. No time to sleep. There was only time "to do." And so she did it. And it was not enough to just make her point, or even to win. She had to find a way to persuade people. She had to change minds. And she did it. By incorporating the insidious principles of manipulation and subtle coercion she uses on Sue and I every day, Lara won her major debate; the proposition of which was that nations really need to stop manufacturing nuclear weapons (One of her best rhetorical blasts was, "Do you realize what just one medium sized nuclear bomb could do the mall in your city?) and convert all those resources into the creation of more and better rock concerts.

Sue and I flew out to Washington to attend the graduation at Georgetown and not ten minutes after Lara received her little trophy, which was made out of a small quantity of enriched uranium by the way, the next phase of the our lives was suddenly upon us: I mean if Winter was all about Winter Formal, and Spring was about Standardized Testing and Celebrities, and Summer was about Nuclear Non-Proliferation, then this Winter – the last winter we will spend together with our wonderful daughter Lara — was all about COLLEGE. Which College?

Sometimes I can't believe that I have been sucked into this pressure cooker called college admissions. But I think I have been. I think I justify it by saying the better the college she gets into the more leverage she will have with her life. I don't think I really believe that, but I, we, behave as if we do. The real determiner of one's future is one's character, and I'm diamond-hard certain about Lara's character. She's got Sue's eyes and her strength of character, and it will do more than any college can to shape her future. And yet, we're doing all the things we're supposed to do to get into a "good" school. Face it: we're like really smart, sophisticated lemmings.

But the process has been going on so long now that we've taken to writing our shopping lists on the back of all the unused college applications that are laying around the house. They're everywhere: in the living room, kitchen, bathrooms. We open a cupboard for a teacup and a brochure from Howard University drops out. We look inside the dresser drawer to find two socks that match and find six reply cards from Temple. We reach back for a few sheets of Charmin and instead grab hold of yet another "life on campus" catalog from Ithaca. Last night, Lara heard a strange noise coming from under her bed, and when she cautiously leaned over to see what it was, she found this guy from Villanova under there. "Just dropped by to make sure you were coming to our open house next week," he said. "And by the way, if you apply today, you'll get a free, three-unit class on Gottfried Leibnitz."

We can't throw the print literature out fast enough, before a new batch arrives in the mail. Apps from NYU, USC, Smith, Syracuse, American University, Boston College, Boston University, Chapman, Fordham, Hofstra, Loyola Marymount; even Stanford, Harvard and Georgetown. And we're going like, what is Harvard doing sending Lara an application; Harvard Petite Boutique, maybe, but Harvard University? I mean Lara is an honors student. She takes nothing but advanced placement classes in U.S. Foreign Policy, Biology, Physics, Cosmology and Phrenology. Compared to wood shop, which I was struggling with at her age and which we called, "industrial arts," her curriculum was super hard stuff. But Harvard was another league ("Ivy" get it?).

After a while though, we figured it out. Harvard wanted her to apply so they could reject her. True! Colleges and universities recruit aggressively; I'd even say irrationally, for students to apply. But they don't recruit to accept kids; they recruit to reject them. The whole point of getting lots of applications is to reject as many as possible. It's taken us a while to figure this out, but finally we're catching on. One of the indicators of a school's prestige is the percentage of kids they accept. The lower the percentage, the higher their prestige. In order to keep that percentage down in the lower realms, they need a lot of applicants. Princeton, for example only accepts 13% of its applicants. If you do the math, that means 98% of them are rejected. Not to be outdone, Yale rejected 100% of its applicants last year. And so Harvard rejected people who hadn't even applied. Not to be outdone, Stanford aggressively rejected the entire state of Texas and anyone who ever watched a NASCAR race. But before they can really do a proper job of rejecting everyone on the planet, these schools have to have a lot of applicants. And that's why we've begun writing our grocery lists on the back of college apps, like just today we wrote one on the back of our app to Purdue: Eggs. Spray Canola Oil. Ground Chuck (I still don't know what this is.) Tomato Sauce. Head of cabbage. Leek. Cilantro. 2 Red Peppers. Fifth of Tequila. Golf Balls. Fifth of Vodka. For Sale signs. 2 Fifths of Whiskey. Half pint of eggnog.

And here's one Lara wrote on the back of her Life at NYU catalog: Close-toed shoes in tennis bag. Tennis bag. Script for *Troilus and Cressida*, Starbucks @ 6:10. GET UP!

We don't know where Lara will be going to school next year. She's got a good academic profile, but short of Ivy League which demands someone who has either gotten all A's, discovered a new element, composed at least one symphony and built lots of houses for poor people in the developing world; or someone like George Bush. Lara, thank the good Lord, isn't like either of those people. She's Lara, and she'll get into the school that is right for her. I, of course, suggested that we home school her for college. I know that's not the way home schooling is usually done, but we've always been innovators in our family, and with college being as expensive as it apparently is (approximately $40,000 per year, plus housing, books and illegal drugs), home schooling through a master's degree seemed like a good idea to me. After all, I could teach her about Liebnitz and Sue could teach her about things like how to be truthful and how to buy mascara on E-bay. I mean what else does one need to know?

But I know what you're thinking.

Will this letter ever end?

MARK MENDIZZA

And the answer is yes. In fact, this is the last Christmas Letter you will ever receive from us. I know I've said that before, but I forgot, and this time I mean it. I swear I'm writing it down in my calendar right now: in '07 only send postcard with big photo of family smiling in front of tree or waterfall. We began our aberrant yuletide epistle a long time ago, and you have been like saints in your patient attention to the story of our twisted lives; from the first poopie in the potty to Lara's first lead role on the Playhouse stage, to her national security campaign to save the malls of the nation from thermo-nuclear destruction. But Christmas and Christmas Letters are for the children, and we don't have that child anymore. We have an Ocho Bonita, a Statesman, an Actor, a Scholar Athlete, a Rock Aficionado, a Tired Teenage Beauty with a long To-Do List. The letter began as a joke, and hopefully remains one, but it was also a way for me to remember moments that I otherwise would probably have just kissed as they passed and then forgot. Yes. This is my scrapbook. Sue remembers moments just by remembering, but I have so many more things to think about than she does, like how gravity works, are there other universes and why Cosmopolitans have become such a popular drink in 2006. So I have to take notes. Which I then send to you.

I'm going to China in January. I should be taking down the big blinking figure of Lara from the roof, but I'm pretty sure I'm going to end up in China: Beijing, Shanghai, Singapore. I'm going with Jessie, a good friend and client from Shimano, to study some of their factories over there and see if I can get a deal on a college. But before I go, we want to thank you from the bottom of our hearts for touching our lives with yours. There is a deep mystery at the bedrock of our being and within that mystery resides the divinity of all things, not just including, but especially

YOU! OK. So you may not be God, but to us you're her envoy. You bear her blessings and you have blessed us, even if by just not telling us what you really think of us. I know this first of all just because I've been around the barn and I know stuff, and second because I've been reading that William Blake guy. He says the only revolution is the one that takes place within the human heart. He says the goal is Freedom and true Freedom comes from Forgiveness and Forgiveness from Love and that's what our Lord Jesus Christ and Christmas is all about. May you love, forgive and be free.

With our own love and regard,

Mark, Sue, Lara and Penny.

2006
Important Events

- **War in Iraq still going strong.**
  Rose Parade drenched in torrential rain for first time in 51 years.

- **Warren Buffett donates over $30 billion to Bill & Melinda Gates Foundation.**
  Lara asks for raise in allowance.

- **Google buys YouTube for $1.65 Billion.**
  Are You Kidding? It only launched last year! Definitely need a raise.

- ***Brokeback Mountain, Borat* and the second *Pirates of the Caribbean* released.**
  Not world historical event like rained out Rose Parade, but "we" like them.

- **Pluto is downgraded from a planet to a dwarf planet.**
  Pluto files suit in federal court; so do dwarfs!

- **Vice President Dick Cheney shoots lawyer while quail hunting in Texas.**
  Since shooting lawyers is not a crime in Texas, nobody cared.

- **Dow Jones closes above 11,000 for first time since June 7, 2001.**
  I mean if this was the nineties we'd be at 20,000.

2007

The Missing Year

2007
Important Events

- **Nancy Pelosi becomes first female Speaker of the House.**
  Lara says, "It's about time!"

- **Steve Jobs announces release of first iPhone**
  Lara says, "It's about time!"

- **To celebrate H.S. graduation, Lara and Kelly take trip to Europe**
  Discover the meaning of cobblestones.

- ***Ratatouille*, the movie, is released.**
  A movie we all watched together, and loved!

- **President Bush announces plan for 21,500 more troops in Iraq.**
  Rumsfeld says, "This is a lot harder than we thought."

- **Dow Jones closes above 14,000, for first time ever.**
  But then, whoa! The recession officially begins:
  Unemployment at 5%; clouds loom.

- **Senator Barack Obama announces his candidacy for President.**
  Hillary says, "Wait a minute! My turn!"

2008

"I'll be Home for
Christmas."

(Found the Missing Year)

Mark, Sue & Lara Mendizza
Orange County, California

December 21, 2008

Dear Yuletiders,

I'm sitting in front of a twelve-inch analog television screen Sue and I installed in the wall of our bedroom fifteen years ago so before going to sleep we could watch reruns of *Cheers, Seinfeld* and *Friends*. It's Sunday morning; or it was Sunday morning before Sue yelled upstairs, "Where's my Tahini!"

Uh-oh. Yesterday I cleaned the refrigerator and threw out the squishy cucumber, the rancid Caesar Salad dressing and I guess I threw out the Tahini, too. It had been there since two Ramadans ago. Sue's making a batch of hummus for Lara. Lara loves homemade hummus, but only with the right kind of pita chips, the ones made by Incas. When I call her "picky," she says she's "discriminating." Sue's making fresh cabbage rolls, too; cause Lara really likes homemade cabbage rolls, as long as the cabbage is from Holland.

"And my bread crumbs!," Sue yells upstairs, again. Darn! "Where are my bread crumbs?"

Double darn! They seemed stale to me, but I guess breadcrumbs never get stale. Or maybe breadcrumbs are stale when

163

you buy them.

By the time I drove down to the store and picked up the Tahini, bread crumbs and pita chips, the morning was over and we had entered what is known as Sunday afternoon.

I'm watching the New England Patriots play the Arizona Cardinals on the twelve-inch screen, and they're playing the game in a fierce blizzard; so can't really tell who's who. The snow is falling so hard that the Patriot's Randy Moss just missed a thirty-five-yard pass from Matt Cassell. The ball touched his fingers and Moss never misses a pass that he can touch. But his fingers were frozen, the ball was wet and a pound heavier than normal. In the stands, instead of doing the wave, fans are throwing snowballs. It's going to be a very white Christmas in Boston, which is awesome unless you're sitting at Logan International Airport waiting to see if your Jet Blue flight is going to be able to take off in the worst blizzard since the Pleistocene era. That's where Lara is: In the Boston blizzard; the freezing, sleety Boston blizzard. She's trying to get home for Christmas. Just like the song.

But wait!

She just called. Looks like her flight is delayed four hours. Instead of arriving here at eight, it will be midnight; if she gets off the ground at all. This is not going to be pretty. She called me a few nights ago. It was eleven p.m. my time, two a.m. in Boston and she'd been studying for finals, a Political Philosophy class taught by a Marxist Polish émigré, in Polish. She'd been in the study lounge below her dorm for several hours, when disaster hit. "I ran out of note cards," she said. She was crunching across the dark, icy Boston sidewalks at two in the morning looking for a store with note cards. She must have suffered a case of Massachusetts brain freeze, which is the only thing I can think of to explain why she would dial home.

"Why don't you just tear up some paper?" I asked, naively. "Write notes on that." "Oh my god!" she said. "Dad. If your note cards aren't all the same size AND color-coded, then . . . well, I don't even want to go there." She was tired. A little OCD'd (obsessive-compulsive disorder). She had a sore throat. She said she wanted to have a family tree trimming event when she gets home, which made me feel good, but which also meant we could be decorating the trees at three a.m. Monday morning. I imagined her walking all alone in the cold, dark deserted boulevard, the ice crackling under foot, her face and fingers numb, looking for note cards on which to jot down her thoughts on the dictatorship of the proletariat, and I had this feeling that seemed so, . . . dialectical: Like Lara's life is as different and as distant from mine as it has ever been, and at the same time she's closer and more familiar than ever. "Do the cards have to be colored?" I asked.

She found a few stores like CVS that were still open, but they didn't have the note cards – or not the colored ones – she so desperately needed, and she had to get back to the study lounge before someone took her spot. "Can't you just borrow some cards til morning?" I asked. "They're like gold, Dad," she said. "If I had a pack of note cards I could sell them for next year's tuition."

The score is 47 to 0, New England, and the only reason to watch the game now is to monitor the storm. For the next twenty-four hours the weather on the east coast is going to affect everything: the hummus, the cabbage rolls and of course Kurt Warner.

You probably don't realize it, but it's been two years since you last received a Christmas Letter from us, and a lot has happened. Think about it: In my last letter I was telling you all about how Lara was taking standardized texts and working up a fake biography in order to get into a "good" college. Since then she's not only become an honor student (Sophomore) at Boston University, she was also named valedictorian at her Traffic School. Back then she didn't even like us very much and today, just two years later, she's like hi Dad, just called to say I love you; Harvard-Yale game's tonight, and then the big charity formal tomorrow. I can wear the same pearls I wore to the charity art opening and the charity fashion show, but I'll need a new dress and shoes for the charity formal. It's for blind kids, Dad. Gotta go. Love you."

I swear, I'm still trying to catch up with all the changes that have occurred. Please! Remind me never to skip a Christmas Letter, again. It's the only way I can tell what's happened to me. That's not true of Sue. She remembers stuff. Like when Lara became a Delta Gamma at B.U. (was it this year?). I thought cool, she's had her genome re-done. Later I found out she had joined a cool sorority that started in 1873. Then I just forgot about it.

Til Sue told me there were dues.

I guess it all goes back to Proust. Remember Proust? *Remembrance of Things Past* (I mean what other kinds of things are you going to remember?) Until Marcel Proust wrote it down in his Christmas letter, it hadn't really happened to him. And that's me, too. I'm a lot like Proust.

THE CHRISTMAS LETTERS II

Some of you even asked what happened to last year's Christmas Letter; not many, but some; one actually. And that is a long story. I did write the letter last year, but so much happened. By the time I finished the footnotes and index, it was February and time to start the letter for President's Day. This year a lot happened, too, but as you know it was really crazy. The whole thing about Obama crashing in on Hillary's coronation, the deep Appalachian lust for Sarah Palin, the collapse of the global financial system, not to mention Sue's six-month sabbatical which calls out for a letter all of its own. I think the best way to gain perspective not only on me, Sue and Lara, but also on many of the dramatic sociological changes that have occurred in our world since Christmas Letter '06 is to actually read the missing letter from last year, and then compare it with how things are this Christmas. That's what a professional would do: Read and compare and then make a career out of describing the paradigm shift.

And there are a lot of reasons this year to go ahead and double up on the page count. First of all, what possible difference could it make? No one's going to read it any way; this year, last year, who cares.

Second, as I have mentioned, Lara at this very moment is curled up with a book on a very uncomfortable bench in the departure lounge at Logan Airport in Boston, waiting for the icy blizzard to pass. I thought that could be a really nice metaphor not just for this Christmas, but for your whole next year: just hunker down and wait for the dark angel of the housing bubble and mindless gluttony to fly over to somebody else's country.

Third, a lot of you are either close to or actually retired. You had kids during your childbearing years, which was smart. But now your kids are gone. Your next cruise to the Galapagos or

Troy isn't til Spring; so why not read a few hundred pages about how Lara dated this guy with a jet; how she became Vice President of Philanthropic Events for Delta Gamma, her sorority at Boston University; Whether or not Lara is going to get home for Christmas. Plus, the pages about finding a toilet in the Forbidden City.

Finally, if you're not retired, there's a pretty good chance you'll soon be unemployed. The point is: curl up on the couch like our dear Lara and read something trivial like "Twilight", "Das Kapital" or the missing Christmas Letter from '07; here's how it began:

Christmas 2007
The Missing Year

Dear Friends, Family and Innocent Bystanders;

They launched Christmas earlier than ever this year. The homes on our street looked like they've been dipped in Skittles. Bing Crosby's posthumous vocals filled the corridors of the nation's malls. And advertisers opened the yuletide flues and let the joyful sludge of Christmas commerce flow into our awaiting holiday troughs. And all this happened in September, before the Red Sox had wrapped up the World Series or Sue had even thought about that new turkey recipe where you soak the bird in a gallon of vodka before setting it on fire in the back yard. Christmas really came early this year.

Of course, it was a matter of national security. The world situation had become so precari-
ous — the large ominous mushroom cloud that
loomed over Iran this week was said by President
Ahmadinajadatneedabhat to be the veil of the
almighty Allah, but George Bush just laughed it
off and said, "No Worries. Heh-Heh. Persian barbeque." Global warming had become so ines-
capable — the 14th floor condominium Sue and
I were going to buy on the Florida coast as an
income property is now happily offered as a 6th
floor condominium; and college football so in-
decipherable — Stanford defeats USC? Oregon
defeats USC? Lara and her girlfriends defeat
USC? — that Americans felt a desperate need
for some kind of consolation, something to sooth
the open wounds of reality, boost the sagging
morale of a people clearly under siege and, yes:
save the nation.

Hallelujah! Just as they have so many times
in our country's history, the American people
stepped up and met the challenge. Instead of
launching an armada on the beaches of Nor-
mandy, however, this time they launched Christmas, like in September!

And it worked. Shopping is the sea on which
the great American economic flotilla finds its
ballast. Shopping is the inerrable calculus that
enables us to know what is true in this crazy

world and what is loss leader. Hey: Shopping tells us who we think we are and, probably most important, it pays for the troops we need to kill people in Iraq.

Yes, we have enemies, even at Christmas. It seems like a law of nature: No matter how cool you are or how many new record labels you come up with, there are going to be people who hate you. And Dick Cheney and Fox News know who they are. When we first thought about writing our 200-page family Christmas letter back in the late 80's, before we even realized it would take 600 pages, I think the Russians, Chinese and Cubans were still our enemies. Before that it had been the Russians, Chinese and Vietnamese. And before that it was the North Koreans. And before that the Germans, Japanese and Italians. And before that, the Spanish. And before that the English. And then the Spanish, again. And then the English once more. And then the French. And before that it was . . . the Cherokee nation. And before that I guess it was the Catholics. And I think that's it.

These were great enemies because they all wore uniforms, which we called "targets." But today our enemies wear sweatpants from Mervyns and since they look just like us, it's a lot harder to tell who's trying to bring us down, or what any of this has to do with the Christmas holidays. Fortunately, the CIA found Intel-R-Us gift cards under the tree, and through a process involving a situation room, a big map and some colored darts, has narrowed our list of enemies this Christmas to three:

- pious people from the Middle East
- poor people from Mexico
- and Hugo Chavez.

After receiving a thorough briefing from his key briefers, the decider-in-chief decided it was time to roll out America's secret weapon: the 75% discount! "Shopping makes us safer," said the decider. "It helps kill our enemies. It stops them at the border. And it keeps them corralled down there in Venezwayland. Christmas, my friends, is war."

Which is why, after promising never to write another Christmas letter, I feel this year it is my patriotic duty. So don't think I don't realize I have once again breached a promise. Every year I say this Christmas letter is the last, and every year I hear the great sigh of relief from both of my loyal readers as they realize that instead of reading about Lara's SAT scores, they'll have a lot more time for redecorating and Sports Central.

As you have probably guessed, Lara has grown up. After sorting through acceptances,

171

rejections and waiting lists from the nation's finest colleges, she decided to go off to Boston University where she plans on studying "Winter," a season she has never experienced out here in Southern California. That leaves Sue and I here alone, trying to figure out what in the hey is going on on Wisteria Lane, and to address yet another life-altering question that every husband and wife in American must eventually face: to which spectator sport do we devote what is left of our emotional lives.

For us, The Christmas Letter lost much of its glow the day Lara joined My Face Space Book, and then of course the roll out of the first iPhone gulped down what was left of her attention to home and me. It dwindled even further when she went to Europe this summer and sent us a postcard from Berlin that said, "I am desperate to live in a place that has cobblestones." Our little girl had grown up and without her here to call me names I felt there was nothing really left to say in a Christmas Letter. It was over. But then, thanks to my therapist – who believes firmly that Santa Claus was a bloodthirsty Nordic warrior — I realized how important Christmas was to our national security.

That's how we began the Christmas Letter '07. It was a little glib. Still priceless, but it had a knowing, ingenious edge that just doesn't seem appropriate for the dire holiday circumstances of

'08. Shopping is no longer something about which one can jest, at least not in public. It's just too important. And our enemies this year have like totally changed. No longer are they the pious, the poor and Hugo Chavez, but instead include domestic terrorists like Bear Stearns, AIG, General Motors, a new terrorist group called The Housing Market, Banks, the SEC and a guy named Bernard Madoff. Wow! Who would have thought just a year ago that a regular New Yorker like Bernard Madoff would turn out to be more of a threat to our national security than Hugo Chavez. Ironic, huh? But it just made us feel so good that Steven Speilberg, Jeffery Katzenberg and other really smart Jewish people could be as stupid as me, and invest all their money with . . . crooks.

That was one of the big sociological shifts from Christmas '07 to '08. In '07 we still believed in Santa Clause. And in '08, we found out he was running a Ponzi scheme.

But wait!

Just got a call from Amanda. She's Lara's secret Santa. She called to see if she could come over and decorate Lara's room before she arrived (if she arrives.) Amanda is a member of the Ocho Bonita, the group of "local" friends – as opposed to Boston friends — who have been together since third grade. Today they're attending colleges all over the country – Amanda and Ali are going to SLO (Cal State San Luis Obispo); Taylor is at UCSB; Deena and Bailey are at Point Loma in San Diego; Kelly's at Berkeley, Kelsey's at University of Colorado, Lisa's some where in South Carolina; and Lara's at Boston University. This is the remarkable thing about Lara's life. First, she's a walking Shamrock.

Since moving to Bean-town, for example (when she was still only seventeen), all the Boston sports teams were suddenly unbeatable. The Patriots were in the Super Bowl during her Freshman year. The Red Sox won the World Series. And need I even mention the Celtics. "You live a charmed life," I told her once, when I needed to borrow money. "The day after you were born the Berlin Wall was torn down and World Communism collapsed. Your Freshman year at BU brought victory to Boston's NFL, MLB and NBA franchises, (which are also Ponzi schemes, by the way). And when nobody else seemed able to, you got tickets to the Yale-Harvard football game. How did you do that?"

"I'm reading 'The Secret', she said, while visualizing really hard about the new dress she needed for that charity formal. Lara's touched by angels (for which I receive a monthly bill) and life gets better for everyone around her. But that's just the charm factor. The really big thing is her address book; better known as "contacts."

Since arriving in Boston and starting her campaign at BU to change the world by ridding it of poverty, blindness and any need whatsoever for math, Lara added six hundred and thirty two people to her telephone list, and twice that to her My Face Space Book page. This doesn't even take into consideration her Twitter, LinkdIn and the Diggs network. During her first semester of her freshman year (from the missing '07 Letter) she auditioned for a musical called FAME and was cast. Sue and I flew out to see her perform and I swear it always just shocks the heck out of me to see her on stage singing and dancing. I remember it was pouring rain in Boston. Sue and I took a cab from the Newberry Street Guest House and as we walked close together, heads down under our shared umbrella, toward the theater, we were surprised at the number of people merging from all sides of the street into the entrance: hundreds of them, and unlike some shows that Lara has been in, they weren't all relatives. A sold-out crowd, which included David De Silva, the guy who developed the original *Fame* on Broadway. She sang and danced like a real singer and dancer, while Sue and I sat in our wet clothes, watching and wondering in awe where she got the guts to get up there and do that! Mitch was there, too; but I can't tell you about Mitch.

This year she was accepted into Delta-Gamma, a national sorority that goes all the way back to Eve. Then, after a lobbying effort that would set new standards for the U.S. pharmaceutical industry, she was elected to the position of Vice President of Philanthropic Events, which is a euphemism for "charity formals." This meant she not only got to organize the charity fashion show for blind kids – which is attended by over three hundred direct descendants of Benjamin Franklin, but also got dibs on the black dress by Carolina Herrera and the Prada clutch.

Yet with all the new friends she has acquired in just a year and a semester at BU – who Sue and I now refer to as associates — Lara and the other original eight girls in the Ocho, have remained as close and steadfast in their friendships as they were back in the six grade when I drove the whole group out at three o'clock in the morning to toilet paper Kevin Physioc's house. Deena, Bailey, Ali, Taylor, Lisa, Kelsey, Kelly and Amanda are back here in the neighborhood for Christmas break, and while Lara sits patient as Paul Revere in the Jet Blue terminal at Logan, Amanda and Taylor are coming over to decorate her room for her return home.

Okay: games over. The final score was 47-7, Patriots. While

MARK MENDIZZA

listening to Cardinal's quarterback Kurt Warner explain to the blond female interviewer on the field that the reason his team lost was because the defensive line of the Patriots had Mongols who are used to playing the game with gangrene, we noticed that the snow in the background had stopped falling. We were encouraged that Lara might still get off the ground. (If she doesn't get out tonight, then she won't be home for Christmas.) And at that very minute we received a text message: "We're boarding!" it said. I thought to myself, charmed life.

So, while we're waiting, let's continue to review Christmas Letter '07 and sift through those cultural differences between this Christmas and last, plus examine the big question facing me at this particular juncture, which is: when do I get the hummus? The problem is the pine nuts. Sue's sprinkled some olive oil, lemon and pine nuts over the top of the mixture and I've been forbidden to mess up the "presentation" before Lara arrives. Someone should do a paradigm shift on this.

The Road to Commonwealth
(2007 continued)

Like many families, we began 2007 in January. By then Lara had already been a senior in high school for a whole semester and pretty much knew everything there was to know, including the name of the person who wrote *Beowulf.* So she was ready to move on. She'd spent first semester studying cosmology and its relationship to the 50% discount, and then slogging through the heavy bog of college applications.

Boy was that an arduous rite of passage.

In ancient times, the rite of passage for young people was like walking on hot coals, carving tribal signs into your cheeks or doing a vision quest. But in 1950, vision quests were outlawed by the Supreme Court by a vote of five to four and replaced by the 800 word personal essay.

"Hot coals would have been a piece of cake compared to this," said Lara, mixing metaphors as she tried to think up three personal qualities that no other seventeen-year-old senior had ever had before, ever! She began her essay with the sentence, "Since I turned green and invented Oxygen I have devoted my life to math and feeding hungry children."

Here's the contradiction. For twelve years, compulsory public education compels a young person to conform to strict, rigid standards. Write like this. Dress like this. Be like this. Then on their college application they drop all that and demand this creative, outside-the-box thinking and non-conformist, all volunteer activities. I mean once you reach a certain level in high school it's just so hard to separate yourself from the herd, because that's what high school is: a herd, including the gifted ones like Lara. Every kid is in honors classes; they're all captain of at least one varsity team, a star in both dramatic and musical theater, a student leader and founding member of the local chapter of Habitat for Humanity.

MARK MENDIZZA

Plus, at parties they quote Lindsey Lohan and Chaucer in the same breath. Lara of course was all this, plus she was our daughter, which was less help getting into college than turning green.

Being a senior in high school is a pretty important stage in life. It lent an intensity to everything Lara did because it was the last time she'd ever do it: like it was her last winter formal, her last Friday night football game, her last performance on stage, her last prom and her last word problem in calculus. For Sue and I it was significant too because it was the last time Lara would ever go to school for free.

Actually, by January 2007, Lara's academic high school career was virtually over because first semester grades are the only ones that colleges want to see before they reject you. So, by January she was done and could spend second semester completely insane about which colleges would accept and which reject her. I have to say that the stress on Lara and her friends was intense, but the tension the kids suffer was nothing compared to the agony with which parents must contend. True, the kids have to compete for a limited number of spaces in the nation's colleges, but the parents have to contend with something much more virulent and destructive: the FAFSA form. **Free Application for Federal Student Aid (FAFSA)**. Sue and I tried to figure out how to complete this form, but after a week

178

and half we'd only reached line six. We abandoned our efforts for aid and just went ahead and began selling our blood.

So, while Lara was organizing a party to help relieve the anxiety associated with colleges that would either accept or reject her, and Sue was advertising our furniture in the Penny Saver, I took a trip of my own.

Mark Goes to China

One of my favorite clients is a company called Shimano. They make the world's finest bicycle components, and like most manufacturers, Shimano has factories in China. My friend Jessie asked if I would like to join him and some European magazine editors on a trip he was making. I figured anything would be better than trying to fill out the FAFSA.

Jessie is unique. There is a ton I like about him: his natural intelligence, his enthusiasm, and his purchase orders. But the thing that always illuminates my own life is his indefatigable adventurousness: Jessie is an adventurer. For some people life is a routine. For some people life is a dream. And for people like Jessie it's an expedition. He travels a lot to Europe, Japan, China. In fact, as I write this letter he's just returning from a recent trip to Cambodia, where he visited a new factory that Shimano had just built. Wherever Jessie goes, he takes his imagination and his bike. He'll get off the plane somewhere like Ho Chi Minh City, and instead of taking a cab to the local Hilton hotel and watching Wolf Blitzer on the big-screen T.V. in his room, he'll assemble his bike and ride fifty miles along the Mekong. On the trip to Cambodia he rode to the Angor Wat, which is a Temple the size of New Jersey. Jessie will take risks – eats foods, meets strange people, smokes things — in order to experience stuff one would not experience without taking them. Needless to say, my trip to China with Jessie was pretty amazing.

Bright Red Roma Tomatoes

I was with Jessie at Shimano Headquarters in Irvine. We needed to book a room for our one-day lay over in Beijing, before catching a shuttle to Qing Dao, the western provincc where the Shimano factory was located.

"Let's not stay in a Hyatt or Intercontinental," said Jessie, as he began to Google hotels. "We're going to China. Let's stay, you know: where the Chinese stay."

No spa!

I'm gazing over Jessie's shoulder at the computer screen, thinking for sure that means, no spa. But I'm game. I've traveled the world, too. I've lived through revolutions. Coups. Police

states. I know how to deal with Kafkaesque Communist clerks. Only back when I was traveling I
had nothing to lose but hair. Now, if I get lost in
China, who's going to help Sue fill out the FAF-
SA form? We looked on-line and found a nice
place that seemed close to Tiananmen Square
and the Forbidden City. It was about sixteen dollars a night, for two; including a nice continental
breakfast that consisted of raw squid and tea.

"Does it have running water?" I asked. "It has
everything," says Jessie. "It'll be an adventure."

After many hours in the air, we looked out the
window of the airplane and saw below a pure
white frozen landscape that curved at the edges
as the earth itself curved. It was breathtaking.
"I think that's Siberia, don't you?" I asked Jessie. "Yeah. I think that must be Siberia." "Looks
cold."

And it was cold.

But cool, too: landing in China.

Our little adventure began when we walked
off the plane and into the crowded area where
people in worn tuxedos hold up white cards with
names of arriving travelers on them. Have you
ever had that, where you walk out of the terminal
and there's like this portly middle-aged guy in a
tattered black suit holding up a card and it has
YOUR name on it. There's really no better feeling
than that.

And even though you know no one is going

to meet you, you still find yourself sort of looking at the names just in case a mistake has been made and someone actually HAS come down to lift your heavy bag off the carousel and drive you to a cool hotel where there's like a buffet in the morning and a nice, lilac fragrant SPA at night. There were lots of cards, of course, but our names were SO not there.

So the first thing you want to do once you arrive in Beijing is to figure out what time it is. Beijing is usually two days ahead of where you left from, or one day after the place you wish you'd gone. We set our watches and then Jessie used his cell to call the hotel. It rang and rang, but no one picked up. We weren't worried though. No problem. It was either eight o'clock at night on either Tuesday or Wednesday and the staff was probably still busy figuring out where they were going to dispose of our bodies.

It was so cold that we actually opened our suitcases, took out our down jackets and slipped them on. While we were zipping up, a guy who looked suspiciously Chinese approached us and asked in pretty good English if we needed a taxi. Ha! And I'm thinking, what does he think we are: Americans?

Outside the big picture windows of the terminal I could see a long line of official yellow communist-looking taxis that were no doubt authorized by one of Mao's grandchildren to drive us safely to the hotel we didn't have. But where's the adventure in that, right? At least that's Jessie's point of view. Instead, he hands the guy the phone number for our hotel and tells him to try and call. While we finished dressing warmer in the terminal, the Chinese guy called our hotel again, but no answer. He says, "Come with me. I take you."

But come on, Jessie and I are way too savvy to be taken in by this obvious scam. Jessie shrewdly smiles back at the guy and says, "How much?" The guy takes out an old, cracked plastic card with some numbers written in Chinese and hands it to Jessie. He takes one look at the shriveled, illegible card and with the world-weary tone of a character out of a John LaCarre novel, Jessie says, "Yeah. Sure. Fine. Let's go."

I can't believe it myself. We're totally alone in Beijing with no contacts, no hotel, and we're following this Chinese guy past the long line of safe, warm communist-party taxis, across the street and into a dark, deserted parking structure where Chinese thugs actually have their second homes. While Jessie continues to dial the number to the hotel we had booked on-line back in Irvine, the guy whistles loudly, scaring the shit out of me. A black, rather beat up,1975 Chevrolet Impala with dark, tinted windows pulls up in front of us. I'm saying to myself firmly, adamantly, I am totally not getting into that car.

The guy opens the door for us, and then puts our suitcases in the trunk. As I get into the back seat I'm wondering when the actual ransom negotiations will begin and what they will use for "proof of life". The guy closes the door and Jessie and I are in a car being driven not by the guy who could speak pretty good English, but by a young female Chinese woman who turns around and smiles at us.

I have to admit, she has a nice smile and doesn't look look too threatening, but you know those Chinese; so . . . indiscernible. She looks a little like Pam on *The Office*, sort of really kind and totally sincere. But that's what people used to say about Mao. And the real question isn't one of ultimate intentions, but rather: can she drive?

Jessie hands her the print out with the address of the phantom hotel and says, with a kind of fake Chinese intonation, "Hotel. You know this hotel?" She smiles like Pam, turns back around and puts the car into third gear. What the Chinese do with first and second gear is one of the great mysteries of the East. The car stutters and sputters and then lunges out of the parking structure and onto the big Beijing expressway that we're both quite certain leads to . . . somewhere in China.

After gaining speed and shifting from third to forth gear, the Impala sputters again and maxes out on the freeway at about forty miles per hour. I think it has something to do with conserving fuel. Jessie and I look out the window and note that its dark, darker than most big cities, and that too I think is because there just isn't as much neon signage along the side of the road as there is in say, Tokyo, or even the cities like New Delhi or Bangkok. China is a rising power, but for most people it is still dirt poor (700,000,000 people still live without a buffet breakfast or a spa.).

After a while the Chinese woman gets on her own cell phone, and we can tell she too is trying to figure out where the mystery hotel is located. Eventually she pulls over to side of the road and stops. She examines the papers Jessie had handed her, and talks more in Chinese into the phone. She nods. And then pulls out into traffic again. But after a while, she pulls back over to the side and stops once again.

This happens several times, and finally she turns and hands the phone to Jessie. The person on the other end of the line apparently speaks some English and now we have a conference call going, in search of the hotel we booked back in sunny California. It becomes clear that the six-teen-dollar hotel doesn't actually exist and finally Jessie says to the young woman, "OK. Forget this hotel. Let's go to another hotel. A different hotel. Tiananmen Square. Hotel by Tiananmen Square. OK?" But she really doesn't understand a word Jessie is saying, and gets back on her cell phone and calls the person who does speak some English. "A different hotel," Jessie says into the cell. "Hotel by Tiananmen Square. OK?"

At this point I feel totally comfortable. The woman driving this car is so kind and trying so hard to help that I'm certain that she is not a gangster or even a member of the communist party. She's . . . well: just like me: totally lost.

We enter the downtown area of Beijing and drive through the city streets for about a half hour, and it is our first glimpse of China. It's very cold, but there are people out on the streets, and little fires glowing from trash receptacles. Lots of vendors and stalls with steamy containers of sautéed sea creatures, bamboo sprouts, bok choi and squid. It looks a little like the cityscape in Blade Runner. The Chinese woman maneuvers the car down dark and narrow alley ways, around some crowded corners and eventually arrives in front of a hotel that is definitely not the Marriot. I mean Marriots aren't located in dark alleys.

I tell Jessie to wait in the taxi while I go inside and see if it's ok. I enter the lobby and right away I'm thinking, for sure, No spa; but at the same time I'm thinking, this is the real China.

And all the people are Chinese. How cool is that? The women behind the desk are dressed in dark blue business suits like airline stewardesses from the 1960s. They are very sharp. Very able. I ask to see a room and they call a bell-boy over to escort me upstairs. The bellboy, whose name is Jun, is dressed in the traditional pseudo-military attire with brass buttons up and down his double-breasted uniform, a little round hat and even epaulets on the shoulders. While going up in the elevator together, he talks to me in a broken English. "Don't pay full price," he says. "They try charge full price, but don't pay full price." I nod and respond knowingly. "You don't have a spa, do you?"

When I return to the lobby I see the female taxi driver had come into the hotel and was sitting at the counter next to Jessie, as if she were a part of our group. I said, "The room's fine." Jessie says, "She came in to make sure we were OK. She just wanted to be sure we were safe."

In the elevator Jun told me that there was no spa, but when I asked about a massage, he said, "Many massage. Many massage." And I'm thinking, Ah-ha!

After our eighteen-hour journey, many massage sounded pretty damn good. Jessie and I changed clothes and met Jun downstairs. He had changed his clothes, too. No longer the bell boy, he was wearing western jeans and a jacket. He escorted us outside and down the cold, dark alleyway. Fifty feet from the entrance to the hotel there was a little storefront with the words "massage" written in English. We stepped up.

We peaked in. Some rather sordid looking Chinese people were sitting in white plastic chairs. They stared back at us like Chinese Children of the Corn. Jessie says, "Is there a better place?" Jun nods down the street.

We continue walking a few yards further and there's another storefront with "massage" written over the door. We walk in. A middle-aged Chinese man in a white shirt is standing behind a counter. He's holding a cigarette between his thumb and forefinger, like in a film-noir movie; A strictly cash-basis kind of guy. He comes out from behind the counter and greets us. He talks to Jun. Then to us. We agree on something like twenty dollars or so. Then we walk through a hanging screen of beads on strings – total film noir — and down some steps to a large room the appearance of which startles me.

First of all, it is brightly lit. Not film-noir at all. On one side of the room there are six massage tables covered in a bright yellow fabric with a blue and red print. These are primary colors, cartoon colors. On the other side, there are six overstuffed lounge chairs with an ottoman at the foot of each one; for foot massages is my guess. The room is bright, neat, clean; nothing like the spa in Rancho Mirage, but tidy. And I don't see any sign of sex. We're in Beijing, not Bangkok; which means much of real life is concealed.

The primary colors gave the appearance of a

child's room. In fact, much of China seems a little childlike to me, at least during the fifteen minutes I have been here. On the other hand, those women behind the hotel desk were pretty hardcore; good English. Polite, but business-like. We paid full price. And of course Mao was no innocent, or if he was, he was like one of those demon-innocents that rule the playground.

What I guess I mean is that all people who have been politically suppressed for a long, long time are inevitably a little hard-edged on the one hand and a little childlike on the other. Development is a different way of relating to power. That's what economic growth is all about.

"Where are the hot rocks?" I ask Jessie. "I need my aroma therapy, my candles and new age music?" "You fucking elitist," Jessie responds.

While I'm trying to figure out whether to take off my clothes, Jessie spots a clean, neatly folded pile of . . . pajamas on top of each of the bright yellow massage tables. I mean I think they're pajamas. They resemble pajamas, cotton bottoms and tops. To me, wearing pajamas for a body massage seems . . . wrong. While I'm thinking about whether I want to put on pajamas that someone else has worn, Jess doesn't hesitate. Even though he's never been in China before, he knows where he is, and exactly what to do. He takes off his shirt and hangs it on a peg on the wall. He takes off his pants. He puts on the pajamas.

Jessie and I are on the massage tables in our pajamas in this brightly lit cartoon-colored room when two small young women from the provinces walk in. These are village girls and as they kneaded and pounded and crawled over the tight contracted muscles in the backs and legs and arms that had given up hope during the long flight across the Pacific Ocean, the Bering Straits, and Siberia, the two of them chatted back and forth as if over lunch. Jessie won't admit it, but he groaned like a dog.

Sam Yee was her name. Two more years massaging fat Chinese businessmen in Beijing, "and then I go home," she said. At the end of the massage, Sam Yee brought Jessie and I a small chilled platter of bright red Roma tomatoes, each with a toothpick stuck into it. "Hey Jess," I said. "Just like a spa."

Mark and Jessie at The Silk Road . . . Bazaar

Next morning, we got up very early. While I was trying to recall exactly what it was that Confucius did say, Jessie was trying to figure out what day it was and why, when he tried to pay for the room the night before, the Chinese woman told him his VISA card was maxed out. "It's my wife," he said. "The minute we took off she bought a new kitchen."

"Go down stairs and find out how we can see Tiananmen Square, The Forbidden City and Olympic Park, plus get those Gucci purses and the Rolex watches." "We have to catch our flight to Qing Dao at like one, right?" "No problem," he said. "But we have to go to the Grand Hyatt first."

Although this is the first time Jessie has ever been in China, he has traveled to a lot of other places and has figured out a quick, fool-proof way to take the measure of the culture in which he finds himself. "You don't go to museums," he said. "You go to the Grand Hyatt. Every city has one and every morning they set up a gigantic breakfast buffet, with like indigenous food on one side and western omelets and bagels and stuff on the other. The quality of the culture is in direct correlation with the quality of the buffet."

It was six o'clock in the morning. Still dark. Still very cold. We caught a cab and drove through abandoned Beijing streets to the Grand Hyatt. It is located on the big main boulevard that seemed typical of almost any large, East European capital city, which was a little weird because we were in Asia. This was the show-case street with large, majestic, grey columned government buildings, embassies and interna-tional hotel chains, the street you'll see a lot of when the Olympics are held here next summer. But in the dark early morning hour it was a little eerie. Very still and weakly lit. Just me and Jessie again, cruising up the empty boulevard, the only two people in China.

The buffet was pretty good; about ten yards of scrambled eggs, yogurt and bagels on one side and on the other another ten yards of pork, noodles and squid (I think Jessie gave it a B). We got all wired up on coffee and then walked in the bitter cold from the Grand Hyatt to Tiananmen Square.

That was one of the weirdest aspects of this already pretty weird trip. The square is vast, gray and flat; maybe twenty football fields in scale, surrounded by monuments and stern institutional buildings devoted to the Chinese Revolution that freed the people from the shackles of a rampant and unjust imperial / colonial / capitalist system and then placed them under the bureaucratic boot of the equally repressive Communist Party. It was so cold that we couldn't feel our faces. There were only a few other people in the entire square, just me, Jessie and some Chinese people all bundled up, scarves wound around their necks and faces. They were in the middle of the square, enduring the icy North China winter, and flying a kite.

That's one of the cool things about coming

here in the middle of winter: you get China all to yourself. "Where are the 1.7 billion people," I asked. "Home in bed," Jessie answered. We were freezing, but we walked out to the center of this enormous field of concrete and just stood there for a few minutes taking in the history and thinking about that solitary Chinese man who, close to this very spot, had single-handedly stopped the entire column of Red Army tanks. We just looked at each other, as if to confirm our presence and our frail grasp on reality.

It surprised me to discover the Forbidden City was right across the street from the square – I figured if it was that "forbidden" it would have been a little further out of town. But there it was, and after getting the "feel" of Tiananmen, we crossed the big boulevard to quickly check out this legendary temple, the corner stone of which was laid down in 1406, way before anyone even thought about creating like, Boston.

As it turned out, the Forbidden City isn't actually "forbidden," it just costs 100 yuen to get in, and the Emperor and his nobles were the only ones with that kind of money.

As we approached the majestic gateway that led from the street into the imperial grounds, we looked up, and over the entrance saw an enormous portrait of Mao Zedong. I have never understood this guy; was he like Stalin? Lenin? Castro? I don't know if you remember, but back in the late seventies after Nixon and Kissinger paid their historic visit to China, Mao was like a folk hero to hairy young western liberals. Kids back then were desperate to get hold of his little red book, from which they would quote little sayings like, "Wash daily" and think that was just about as deep a saying as they'd ever heard. Then Mao would like execute all his enemies, many of whom were close family members, or make one of those "great leaps forward", which for most people meant a leap to forced labor and a new life in the concentration camp, and young people in America would amass onto Wilshire Boulevard and, holding up their red books, they'd cheer, "Grow your own fruits and vegetables."

Today, of course, those same people slide their AARP cards through movie box office windows across the country, stating firmly, "Two seniors for Jackie Chan, please."

I just never got that whole Mao thing. And then there's the mole? Even in the thirty foot portrait over the entrance to the Forbidden City, his portrait had a big mole on his left cheek, which I felt he should have had removed. I mean if you're going to rule with an iron hand over 1.5 billion people (1.7 billion today), you should pay some attention to your appearance. Since then, however, I've learned a lot more about culture; that cultures like ours would have the mole removed, while others would like write poems about it.

Once inside the gates of the Forbidden City, Jessie and I spent most of our time looking for a place to pee. After the buffet and all that coffee, we really had to go bad. "What's the word for bathroom?" I asked Jessie. For the first time on our trip, he looked worried.

We walked up to one frozen Chinese person after another, each one offering us a choice between a bobbing-head Mao doll or a Kit Kat bar, and we'd say, "Bathroom?" in a perfect Chinese accent. They'd just stare at us. Then we'd walk up to another person in a shop where they were selling 2008 Olympics dolls and we'd say, "Wee-wee" which, depending on your inflection, means either what's that on your nose or gotcha! We tried leu, john, throne room and crapper, but no one understood what we were talking about. I turned to Jessie and told him if we didn't find a toilet on the next try, I was going to act it out so there would be no misunderstanding about what we were looking for. "You mean point to your thing?" he asked, very concerned because he knew how sensitive the Chinese culture is to things. "I'm going to squirm and point and say . . ."

"Toilet!" he said, loudly. "Toilet," I repeated. "That's it! Why didn't we say toilet fifteen minutes ago?" "I know," I said, shaking my head and plunging my hands deep into my pockets. We walked up confidently to another frozen Chinese guy who was selling little red Mao books and said, "Toilet!" like really seriously. He bowed and then pointed toward a far-off horizon. "Toilet in Shanghai," he said, which was over a thousand miles away.

Having absorbed the cultural riches of the Grand Hyatt, Tiananmen Square and The Forbidden Palace (remember, we have to catch a plane to Qing Dao Province at one o'clock), next we pulled out our map and located the Silk Road Shopping Bazaar, where all the great European designers from Chanel and Gucci to Prada and Fendi offered their $2,000 bags for six dollars each. This is the thing about Chinese culture that I think most intrigued Sue and Lara. I mean they were all about the Ming, and had a deep affection for the Qing Dynasty, too; but the ability of the modern Chinese merchant to sell a Burberry bag for under twenty dollars was . . . like way better than the invention of Taoism, and put the discounts at Bloomingdale's to shame, (even if the bags were made out of old newspapapers).

Of course it was Jessie who got us there. "Let's take a cab," I said, sensibly. "Cab!. We don't need no stinking cab!" And I'm going like, Beijing underground? Are you kidding.

We walked down the stairway outside the Forbidden Palace to a cold and surprisingly vacant underground platform. Jess and I had been the only ones in Tiananmen Square and we were the only ones on the platform, too. (Later I found out most of the 1,700,000,000 people in China were practicing for the opening ceremonies of the 2008 Olympics. Attendance was mandatory and anyone who messed up was totally condemned to like a "great leap forward.")

I don't know how he does it, but Jessie just walked up to one of those maps with the maze of colored lines that looked like a close up of Mickey Rourke's bloodshot eyes, and found the box that said, in Mandarin Chinese characters, "You Are Here."

Of course, I've been on undergrounds all over the world – London, Paris, New York, Madrid, Munich, Bucharest — but no matter what train I picked, I always ended up in Trenton, New Jersey. Jessie's different. He has a sixth sense I've seen operate more than once. It kicks in most intensely when he's really, really cold. Standing before that map, he was weighing two things: did we have time to get on over to the Silk Road Bazaar and still make our flight to Qing Dao, and what would happen if we skipped the bazaar and returned home to our wives without one of those $10 purses. He stares at the map for a while, looks up the dark empty track, thinks about arriving home without a purse, looks back at the map, shifts the weight of his backpack, and says, "this way."

On the train we finally did see some Chinese

people, but they looked SO cold and forlorn. Heads down, swaying back and forth, wishing they were in L.A. — I think I saw Michael Cimino in the back, all bundled up in one of those traditional, quilted Chinese jackets, holding his little rice bowl in his lap. And for a minute I felt a deep compassion for the people of China, for the relentless conformity they were forced to endure and of course for the alphabet they were forced to learn, especially the letter "b". To a God I'm not even sure about, I said silently, thank you lord for birthing me on top of the San Andreas Fault.

I followed Jessie off the train, up the stairway and on to the enormous building that housed the Silk Road Bazaar. In case I haven't mentioned it, I've been to bazaars – Tangier, Tehran, Fez, Istanbul, Jeddah, Bankok, even the swap meet at the Rose Bowl, where I bartered with some strange looking people from the city Bellflower – but nothing like this. It seemed about the same size as Tiananmen Square itself, only there were like five floors. Aisle after aisle after aisle of designer clothing, watches, and of course handbags by Michael Kors, Jimmy Chu, Salvatore Ferragamo . . . everyone.

"Two for twenty dollars," says one guy. "You want Rolex? Three for five dollars." I know we've all heard about these knock-offs before, and a lot of them are on the streets of L.A. and New

York right now, not to mention the wrists and shoulders of society's wannabe elites, but to witness the orgy of unlicensed merchandise on this scale was . . . tempting: you just wanted to pull up a truck and fill a container with the stuff and take it all back home and turn it into "tuition." "Let me see your phone," I said to Jesse.

The importance a women's handbag has in her life cannot be exaggerated. It's huge. A woman who feels good about her bag marries well and has kids that grow up to own their own production company. The ones who feel bad about their bags marry guys who change their own oil, and when the divorce is final, the kids want to live with the neighbors. I remember the night before Jessie and I departed for Beijing. Still trying to figure out how to write the letter "b", I couldn't sleep very well, and around two in the morning I got up. As I was walking back to bed I saw a bright full light coming from Lara's room. Thinking she had probably fallen asleep while reading the Henry James masterpiece, "Do They Wear High Heels in Heaven?," I opened the door and looked inside her room. I was surprised to see Lara sitting up in bed, leaning against her headboard with her laptop on her lap. She looked up at me.

"What are you doing up?" she said. "It's two-thirty" "I couldn't sleep," I said "Still can't find Qing Dao on the map." "Could be an old map," she said, wisely. "Yeah, but I think it's an old province." "Did you find China?" "Yeah. Yeah. You know the only thing I can say in Chinese is, Kung Pao?" "Dad. Stop worrying. They'll speak English." "Yeah. You're right. It's China. They'll all speak English. And I'm good at that. What are you doing up?" "I just downloaded pictures of the purses I want you to buy. If you want me to succeed in life, I need at least two of these."

From one of the crowded aisles of the Silk Road Bazaar, I dial Lara's number. "Hi honey. This is Daddy. I'm in Beijing. Yeah. I'm here with Jessie. Yeah. He's fine, too. It's cold here. And everything's beige." "You know, that's why they call it Beijing," she said.

"Ha. Ha. Yeah, I just want to make sure I get the right purse; you wanted one Coach and one Chanel, right? The Chanel clutch? There are five floors of knock-offs here and I want to make sure I get the right one. Okay. Okay. Like the one you printed out, right? Yeah. It's $3500 at South Coast Plaza and only six dollars here. So it's a pretty good deal. Yeah. Okay. I'll get two. Tell Mommy I found the Tods she wanted. A little more expensive though, like two for fifteen dollars. This guy looks hungry, though. I'm going to try and get him down."

"No. That's okay. Yeah. We pretty much found out everything there is to know about China. Very cold. No one here during the winter.

Yeah. We saw, like Tiananmen Square and the Forbidden Palace and the buffet at the Grand Hyatt, but we won't have time to see the Great Wall. Did you know they built it like 700 years ago to keep out illegals? And hey, the Chinese invented paper, too. Did you know that. Yeah, but America invented the three-hole punch. We have to catch a plane to Qing Dao. You didn't by any chance find Qing Dao on that map did you? No? No, me either. Maybe I'm spelling it wrong. But Jessie's here. He'll find it. Okay, we have to go. Love you, honey."

The Magnificent Twenty-three

On the plane to Qing Dao Province, which turns out to be right there on the east coast, across the Yellow Sea from the Koreas, Japan and Taiwan, I turned to Jessie. "They spelled it wrong," I said. "Look. They spelled it, 'Tsing-tao.'" "That's the Mandarin spelling," he replied, as if that cleared everything up." "Got it," I replied. "How far is the Shimano factory from the airport?" I asked. He booted his computer and looked at the itinerary. "About three and a half hours. We're taking a bus." And I'm thinking, like three days to get to a shoe factory. Maybe we should have kept some manufacturing "on-shore," just in case we needed to actually get some shoes.

Not long after landing in Qing Dao/Tsingtao, while Jessie and I were standing in the terminal talking about how to make a better wheel (seriously), European guys begin showing up one after another. First there were these two French guys; thin, looked like jockeys. "Bon Jour, Simon. Bon Jour Mathieu." They greeted Jessie as if they were best friends. Then there were two Italian guys; trim, energetic. Ciao! Ciao! Maurizio, Simone. Tim Gerrits from the Netherlands, Jessie's Shimano counterpart in Europe. Germans: Karl, Matthias, Florian, Jurgen and Uwe. I was so grateful to Karl for looking older than me, that I gave him a Rolex. Gradually these individuals from all these different cultures began to fuse into a cohesive, goal-oriented group, like in the movie, *The Magnificent Seven*. They talked about cycling, the races, the bikes, the world at large. I decided that in a lot of ways, I resembled an elder Steve McQueen.

Guys from Spain. Ole! Adrian, Jose! Tall, worn, disheveled guy from Sweden, hey Pars. Three guys from England: Neil, William and Steve. They're pulling luggage on loud trundling wheels. They're cohering. They're writers, editors and photographers from European bicycle magazines. They're very likeable, mostly young and worldly and poor. The bike itself is a unique form of transportation that just naturally improves the well-being of the rider and of the world. Bikes don't fuck up the air and suffocate the earth. The bicycle used to be a primary mode of transport in China, but no more. There are still a lot of people pedaling about (usually with surgical masks covering their faces), but today they're way outnumbered by scooters and automobiles. Isn't it ironic that the people of China are trying desperately to rid themselves of non-polluting bikes and replace them with toxic automobiles, just as the Europeans and some Americans are seeing the wisdom of having air?

A guy from Finland, Janne. Quido from Holland (I know. I thought it was an Italian name, too). Two guys from Korea show up; Byeong-Ho Son, whom they call BH, and Sang-Jae Lee, whom they call Larry. They're from Wooyan, a Korean footwear company in which Shimano purchased an interest so that it could control the manufacturing of their own stuff, instead of outsourcing it. Shimano is unique in that. Masterful engineers. Meticulous manufacturers.

As you can see, the group is getting bigger, and decidedly more diverse. It's one of the things I like about cycling: so clean, silent, global and diverse. So benevolent, really.

I guess we're going to bus it to Lianyungang, which is a city in Qing Dao/Tsingtao where Shimano has some of its factories (together with Wooyan) for manufacturing components, shoes and cycling wear. Yes: it's basically a press junket. In addition to my role as an "adult" – I mean these people are so young, I'm also there as a writer, someone who will go back and write about Shimano's advanced technologies in footwear, pedals and wheels.

TK and Tanaka show up, two Japanese representatives from the company who seem more out of the *Seven Samurai* than the McQueen movie. They walk up with smiles that are both enthusiastic and restrained. Their gracious bow brings order to the group. TK gestures toward the parking lot and the Americans, Europeans and two Koreans gallop toward the bus like the Magnificent Twenty-three.

Lianyungang seemed more alive to me than Beijing. It was a bustling little place with lots of people, cars, scooters and bikes. Maybe it's the location. I mean it's right there on the east coast of China, across the Yellow Sea from Korea, Japan and of course Taiwan. I'm guessing, but it would seem like a perfect vector for a confluence of factory construction; where all that Japanese and Korean brainpower and drive could converge with imported raw materials and inexhaustible manpower from China to create like billions of Barbie Dolls. When I got up the next morning and pulled back the curtains I looked out on a large square around which scooters, cars and bikes were already circling, and in the center of which a group of about thirty people were practicing the serene, rhythmic movements of some serious Tai Chi.

When our group entered the factory floor I felt I had finally walked through the gates that led to the "real" China. Think of the Great Plains of North America. Now instead of golden fields of corn and wheat, think of row after row of a gillion pulsating sewing machines, assembly tables and automated mechanical devices lined up all the way from Kansas to Canada, each one manned by a young Chinese girl in a blue smock, head down, eyes focused, intensely concentrated on cutting, sewing, drilling, gluing, inspecting, or . . . That's what it was like: a vast plain of anonymous, repetitive motion exerted by hundreds of diminutive young girls with fingers so delicate and deft, and an intelligence so swift, that it was almost as if they were created to insert a row of tiny eyelets or attach the carbon-fiber sole onto the upper panels of Lance Armstrong's racing shoes. It was a little like the Silk Road Bazaar: you hear about all this stuff, but when you witness it first hand, it has a much greater impact on your . . . conscience.

When you think about today's China you can think about the upcoming '08 Olympics and the recent manned space flight, maybe the Shao Lin Monks and even the ironic fact that the Chinese Communist Party owns a second trust deed to most of America. But what's at the core of all this

Chinese success? What enabled them to buy up all those Treasury notes? Follow the trail of two decades of Sino-economic success a few steps down the ladder, closer to its source, and you end up on the factory floor, watching these girls (some guys) working 10-12 hours a day, six days a week, for about $125 per month, including room and board. When the scene before my eyes connected with those numbers inside my head – $125 per month! – I grokked China.

The $125 per month is what attracted every manufacturer in the industrialized world to lay off its workers, close shop and move off-shore. The ability – and training – of these girls to assemble Barbie dolls, Nikes and micro-chips for a small fraction of what it would cost in a country that enabled its citizens to have cars, lawns and more than one set of clothing is what enabled the Chinese to win the rights to the '08 Olympics, put a man into space and take the Shao Lin Monks on tour.

Of course there was some intellectual equity at work, too. The Japanese partnered with the Koreans (Europeans and Americans in this equation are little more than sales and service personnel); they provided the information (engineering) necessary to make the shoes. And information is valuable. In fact, there are some people (a lot of them are on my team, part time, or working on the Large Hadron Collider in Geneva.) who speculate that "information" is actually the foundation of the universe, that software (mathematics) will ultimately surpass hardware (matter) as the essence of existence. I don't know how you get a shoe or a big HD TV out of it, but personally I'm looking forward to finding out. Because if that's the case, I have just a shit load of information I'd like to trade in for some tuition money. Yet in terms of corporate dividends, treasury notes and the quest for dominance, the inverse law of labor costs—the less it costs the more power you have in the market – is like God. And these girls work for $125 a month.

Alas, the Magnificent Twenty-Three were not there to free the villagers from a gang of abusive outlaws—because Shimano treated the girls quite well. Life in the village would have been much, much harder. We ate the same fish and rice they did for lunch and it was great. Every hour, the machines stopped and a slightly martial-style of music filled the factory. The girls stood up next to their workplace and for ten minutes they did a series of callisthenic exercises in time to the music. When the music stopped, the machines re-booted, and the girls sat down and continued their work.

By world standards, they were doing well; sort of where immigrants to the U.S. were around the turn of the nineteenth century, only with a lot better work environment and safety standards.

No. Our noble band of journalistic Samurai was not there to rescue the oppressed, but to observe them.

We photographed, filmed and interviewed. We took notes. Over lunch we spoke knowingly about cultures, exchange rates and QC standards. At night we visited the city. Still bustling with life—it was in Lianyungang that I witnessed the emerging Chinese middle-class that would someday help us bear the burden of a crazed, superficial consumerism — Jessie, TK, Tanaka, BH and I walked about in the cold. Lots of shops were lit up and open; couples, families were picking up items for dinner, just like all the rest of the world at six and seven o'clock. I was still exhausted from my bargaining at the Silk Road Bazaar and asked if we could get some coffee.

"Maybe tea," said BH. Hey! Yeah. Tea in China.

Although a Korean, BH lived in Lianyungang and in a way was our gracious host. He escorted us into a tea house just off the main fare and it was a very cool place. Kind of dark, natural woods, men on stools playing the game of GO. We sat down at a small table. A waitress walked up and greeted us, then handed us menus, tea menus. Menus with like twenty-five different loose-leaf teas. TK and BH helped us make a selection. Then we got up and walked over to the condiment bar which consisted of maybe twenty small open wooden barrels each of which contained an offering of nuts, dried fruit, sweets and, worldly as I was, a lot things that I could not name. You took a plate and placed a small portion of whatever little snacks happened to appeal to you. Then you went back to the table and while waiting for your tea, began cracking nuts and savoring unique combinations of tastes. The tea was served in tall glasses. The loose-leafs rested at the bottom of the glass and you poured hot water over them. Then you sipped and nibbled and talked business.

On the last night in Lianyungang our hosts prepared a large feast for their western guests. Of course, being generous, gracious hosts was as important in Chinese, Korean and Japanese culture as it was everywhere else in the world, except of course Southern California where it is considered a nuisance. The Germans, French, Italians, Dutch, Swedes, Belgians, Brits and me and Jessie sat with our Korean and Japanese friends around large round tables that had kind of a Lazy-Susan-type device in the center. The food was placed on the swiveling circle and then you just turned the thing around to get your soups or pork with bok choi or various kinds of squid-like items. The food just kept coming, and coming and you had to watch your Asian neighbor very carefully to figure out what to eat and how to eat it. Frankly, I'm not very good at

MARK MENDIZZA

eating in public, even when its something easy like pancakes. And though I've eaten stuff on ten of the world's twelve best-known continents, I have to admit that I was a little overwhelmed by the sheer quantity and variety of foods which of course I had to eat with a pair of sticks. I was tempted to play a Chinese version of Wheel of Fortune, just spin the thing and see what showed up in front of me, but that's apparently frowned upon. Alas, very little of the food ever actually reached my mouth.

After dinner Tanaka stood up and offered us three options for the rest of the evening. "You can have a massage. You can go to Karaoke. Or you can go to room and sleep." He went around the table getting each of us to express a preference, and then he wrote it down on a little piece of paper so he could report our whereabouts to the communist party. And that decision too, like eating things that seemed a lot like rubber, placed a lot of pressure on me. I wanted desperately to go back to my room and sleep, but, trying to keep up with all these youthful Europeans, I didn't want to seem like the old guy. Jessie of course, being as gregarious as he was drunk on all the obligatory toasts, said he wanted to go to Karaoke. When Tanaka came to me, I paused and almost said sleep, but then suddenly found myself saying, "Oh yeah: Karaoke. I mean "I feeeeel good!"

Why do I do that?

It's a proven paradigm that pre-historic ancestors who walked back to the cave alone after a big communal feast, got eaten. The ones that did Karaoke and then walked back with the group, survived. Groups protect you. If you want to survive, I reasoned, you got to Karaoke.

When I got back to the room to brush my teeth I re-thought the whole paradigm and realized it was a bunch of shit. I was old. I'd traveled fifteen thousand miles in a couple days, without a Starbucks. I called Jessie and said, "Dude. (remember: this was January 2007, so you could still say "dude") I'm staying home." "You're such a fucking girl," he replied. But with the Italians and Spanish safely out of earshot, what did I care?

In the morning I pulled back the drapes and looked again at the Chinese people finding their "chi" down below. I admired that, taking the time to find their "chi" in the morning, before taking over the whole fucking world in the afternoon. I called Jessie to see if he wanted to join me for breakfast. When I heard his voice, I could tell he was very, very sick. "I Karaoke'd all night," he said. "I lost my voice. I have a fever." "You caught something, dude. Were there girls there?" "Yeah. But they were just hostesses. They just sat with you and made sure you were ordering drinks." "For sure, Jess: You have Karaoke Disease. Do you have any antibiotics?"

I went downstairs. The Magnificent-Twen-ty-Two were having breakfast. I sat next to Jose from Spain. He too had gone to Karaoke and he too had the disease, some kind of gurgling green shit inside of his chest, and a throat the color of a Southern California sunset. I told him Jessie was infected, too. He didn't care about Jessie. Over breakfast, he told me about the Ka-raoke girls. It was a little strange, because he felt some outrage that the young women had been forced to drink with him, to dance with him, even to sing with him, almost against their will. I think he felt it was immoral, not so much on her part, but on the part of the men who had forced her into that position and of course on his part for participating and paying for it with a bad case of Karaoke Disease. Being a few decades older than Jose I explained to him as gently as I could that men were pigs. "I've lived in many countries among many different people from many differ-ent cultures and the one thing I found them to all have in common is their love of music and the men are pigs." Jose nodded, and thanked me.

During the long bus ride to Shanghai we stared out the big windows at mile after mile of grey, fallow fields and leafless trees, broken up by small dim villages in the distance. While be-ing lulled by the drone of the bus engine and the muted din of different languages from my fellow travelers, I slipped into an altered state of consciousness and gained yet another insight into the mysteries of Chinese culture: paint. There's no paint.

I mean sure: the Forbidden Palace is painted. The Peking Opera is brightly colored. But out here in the country, they build block-style concrete buildings to house the 1,700,000,000 people, and then they forgot the last part. There's no paint. No trim. In Austria all the villages are painted and there are little flower boxes under each window. But in China all the housing is this sad, totalitarian cement-grey color that just screamed out for a consultant. At some point I think China will have it's own equivalent of the nineteen sixties. The people will demand their freedom, and then they too will discover tie-die, psychedelics and the power of brightly colored polyester. But that's way down the line. For now, it's still all about getting some food to eat, compulsory economic growth and social control.

It seemed like every mile on the long junket to the city of Shanghai, Jessie got sicker and sicker. By the time we reached the banks of the Yangtze, he was just all fucked up. The plan had been to fly from Shanghai down to Singapore where we'd take another bus to yet another of Shimano's factories, this one just across the border in neighboring Malaysia. I remember Jessie and I sitting in the Shanghai airport. He looked like Freddie Kruger. Our flight south was just getting ready to board when I said to Jessie, "Go home. You don't need to go to another factory. You've been there. You're sick. When they see what you look like they probably won't let you into the country anyway. I mean Singapore has very strict requirements. People with Karaoke Disease are turned back at customs."

He flipped open his cell, and called United. He booked a flight: Shanghai-Hong Kong-LAX-John Wayne. In just eighteen hours Jessie would be home in bed, while I, on the other hand, would be dressed in a colorful floral print shirt – a gift from our Malaysian hosts —, sitting at yet another banquet table with Tanaka, Uwe and Pars, watching five Malaysian girls perform a classic Malaysian folk dance for what remained of the weary but nonetheless Magnificent Twenty-Two. We were talking to Tanaka about labor costs and I found it almost humorous when he leaned towards me. "The days of cheap labor in China and Malaysia are over," he said. "We're going to Cambodia."

That was January of 2007. Since then we have watched the world's financial Titans carrying their office plant and desk accessories out of the building in a cardboard box, leaving Obama to clean up the mess, which it looks like he's going to do. Subprime or not, as Jessie would be the first to tell you, life goes on. After recovering from that nasty case of Karaoke Disease, he was back to his peripatetic ways and recently touched our lives once again with his warm and worldly wisdom, just when we needed it most.

Cheers

We were in Boston with Lara, helping her move into the dormitory at Boston University, where she would be going to school for the next four years.

It was an emotional time. We were dropping our daughter off in a state that was not only 3000 miles away, but also one that had what they called "winter." On top of that, our precious little girl was going to be living in a city with traditions that go all the way back to the American Revolution; whereas our traditions out here in California only go back to about eleven o'clock this morning. Every block in downtown Boston has a cemetery that contains the remains of Benjamin Franklin. Every building has a brass plaque that says George Washington convened the Revolutionary Army at this very corner, and bought snacks from the guy across the street. Every family up on Beacon Hill descended from Johnny Tremaine, even though he was a fictional character from a novel written by Ester Forbes in 1943. The point is that these people are so full of tradition that whenever they sit down to have dinner they often feel an deep historical compulsion to wear shoes. "Winter" and dressing for dinner are new for Lara. And as if that weren't enough, the Governor is a Republican, whose name is Mitt. In this strange land of Mitt, brick, cobblestones and winter, Lara would begin her journey from the realm of free public education to one that costs as much as the International Space Station.

We'd spent the day with Lara and her new roommate Lizzie. Unpacking all her stuff and finding a place to put it was like trying to fit the U.S. 1st Armored Division into a rented storage unit. It was good that we were so busy, though, because below the hectic, bantering surface was a deep and abiding sadness about leaving our Lara alone here in Boston. It was almost unreal. Something strange was happening to our lives, something psychologists have come to call the "tuition-syndrome" and it was the urgent, trivial tasks like making a trip to CVS for another roll of duct tape, or to Radio Shack for a computer cable, that kept me and Sue from just sitting down on the dormitory floor and crying. Lara felt it too, I'm sure. Although she didn't show any real signs of anxiety – she rarely does – we knew she must be feeling all the mixed emotions that we were feeling. In fact, in the few short months that led up to our departure for Boston in late August, Lara herself had changed; I mean it was almost as if she liked us.

We'd had dinner the night before at a popular outdoor restaurant on Newberry Street. It was a warm night. The street was bustling, and while I was pointing out to Sue and Lara how many of the Bostonians were wearing shoes, I suddenly had this realization that Lara was not just growing up (she was, but come on: she was still only seventeen), but that she had somehow made a quantum leap and was in many ways, not just my contemporary, not just becoming a peer, but was actually making her way ahead of me. (Something Lara herself had known for many years.) Her mind was so quick, so deft with everything including all these new people she was meeting and this new strange place that was to become her home. I had to make an effort to break through the melancholy that kept falling over me; the ache caused by the inevitability of Lara simply walking out of our lives. Even though I had thoroughly accepted and even desired it at times, as the reality drew closer, her departure became a sad, ominous thing inside of us. "It's like the last supper," I said. "Tomorrow at six o'clock we have to say good bye."

The feelings peeled off in different directions. I think Sue and I both felt a profound and painful separation that I compare to losing your keys. But there was also a feeling that was like being re-born, like everything was suddenly all new and unknown. Instead of just talking about my waistline, we found ourselves talking about life and politics. It was different. Out there on Newberry Street, Lara sat poised and confident and the three of us were having a fun, nuanced and meaningful conversation about the Lewis and Clark Expedition, and I swear I found myself thinking, when did she become so knowing? At one point I asked Lara who she was going to vote for, and instead of just saying Obama (who she's leaning toward) she analyzed the candidacy of Obama, Clinton and Edwards with such sophistication and insight that I found myself changing my own opinion — which, as you know, is my most prized possession.

The next day began the countdown to six o'clock. In our hotel room we had packed the sixty suitcases that made up her trousseau for freshman year. After zipping up the duffel and looking around the room one more time for the lost curling iron, it was time to call the cab. For me, that was an emotional moment. No more traveling, no more dinners, nothing left to distract us from the fact that soon we would make the drive to BU and Lara would disappear from our lives into her own. Picking up the phone and saying to the desk clerk, "Could you get us a taxi" was for me like crossing the threshold from our past life to our future; from childhood, in a way, to . . . the brave new world of Commonwealth Avenue. We were in launch mode now, crossing the Rubicon and nothing would be the same ever again.

The taxi driver was a stout middle-aged guy from Israel who'd been driving taxis in Boston since like before the Six-Day War. He helped us get the freshman trousseau into the back of the big van cab and during the drive to BU his running commentary was a welcome distraction. Pointing to a portion of the BU campus he said, "Over there I used to watch the Boston Braves play baseball." (The Boston Braves became the Milwaukee Braves which became the Atlanta Braves which I think are soon to become the Braves of Azerbaijan). Then he pointed to Fenway Park on the left and you could tell he was proud of what the Red Sox had accomplished in the last few years. From her dormitory, Lara would practically be able to see the field. While making a u-turn on Commonwealth Boulevard to maneuver us up to the curb in front of the dorm, the Israeli said, "You know there will never be peace in the Middle East because those people still live in medieval times. They don't want to change." And I'm looking at Lara and going, like who does?

I waited outside with the small mountain of bags while Sue and Lara went inside to get the key and big cart the school made available to help transport Lara's stuff up to the 13th floor where her dorm room was located. Other families with even more luggage than we had also pulled up to the curb and unloaded. Boston cops were standing by, observing an annual ritual that must have been as boring for them to see as it is for you to read: parents turning their children over to the city of Boston for their transition from adolescence to adulthood.

And believe me I realize how boring it must be. I mean sending your kid to college is about as common as sending your kid to war. But like having a child in the first place, which people have been doing since the fifties, it's old and new at the same time: old for you, but like space travel for us. So just keep reading and be thankful I've decided not to include the part about laundry.

The dormitory reminded me of the army barracks I was housed in at Fort Dix, New Jersey where for three months I was trained to "kill without mercy" (they actually made us yell that during bayonet training). It was very hectic, with kids from all over the country schlepping their stuff up and down the elevators and pretending to be cavalier about the fact that they're going to be sharing a room with a person who is not only from a smaller state, but who doesn't have any idea how cool you were in high school.

When we reached Lara's room, we met Lizzy and her mom. Her Dad was there, too, but he was under the bed, trying to assemble what they call rack risers, which are complex mechanical devices that raise the bed two feet off the ground so you can store all your stuff underneath it. It was hot, humid and chaotic as the Moms and girls unpacked and the Dads . . . well Lizzie's Dad, spent most of the afternoon under the bed with his tool box. I stood around day dreaming about Johnny Tremain, until someone would say, "More hangers! We need more hangers." And then I'd go get the wrong kind of hangers.

This went on for several hours during which we found out that Lizzie and her family were from Chicago. He was in software. She was a para-legal. And Lizzie was pre-med, until the first week of school, that is; when she discovered that a medical degree required one to actually touch internal organs; ewwww! She switched to Communications.

This was not the first time Lara and Lizzie had met. They became acquainted during the BU orientation that had taken place back in June. They had liked each other so much that they'd decided to try and become roommates. So they'd been text messaging and communicating on My Space Face Book or whatever for months. In fact, Lara had already formed a core group of probably ten or eleven people in Boston that she was in touch with electronically more or less night and day. To me, this was amazing, that she already had a dozen friends in Boston when I didn't have half that many in the city I've lived in for thirty years. Lizzy was a great young person and we felt comforted by the fact that Lara and Lizzie were the same size and could share clothing. But it didn't alter the uneasy fact that soon, in just a few minutes actually, we'd be saying good-bye to Lara and starting our new life as a hysterical, purposeless couple.

The moment came rather suddenly. One minute we were all scurrying around trying to figure out how to get the Skype software to work so we could at least see Lara's face on the computer once in a while. And the next minute it was six o'clock, and the girls had to go to a meeting. Wait a minute. I'm not ready. I can't get Skype to work. I think we need more hangers.

But time is as merciless as a high school assistant principle and soon Sue and I were standing there in the little dorm room, watching Lizzy hug her parents and say goodbye. Then we watched Chrissy from down the hall say goodbye to her parents. And that left us, me and Sue and Lara. Everyone was holding back their feelings and their sobs, trying to be strong for one another. And then Lara was in my arms. I held her as if I would never see her again. I felt a wave of love come over me like a controlled substance. I pulled back and looked into her eyes, which had reddened and filled with tears. Mine, too. Everyone's. This was a song that went all the way back to kindergarten when we watched Lara walk away from us and enter the classroom where we would no longer be there to protect her. She was the world's now, in the hands of God and BU. The moment arrived and departed in one long agonizing heartbeat. And the next thing you know, Sue and I were alone in the dorm. It was silent. Lara was gone.

We sat down on chairs in the little study lounge looking at the pale-yellow cinderblock walls. One of the hard things about leaving Lara here in Boston is that she had all of a sudden transformed from a high school person who really didn't want too much to do with parents, into this most beautiful, eloquent and even likeable person; like someone I want to see more of rather than less. "All of a sudden, she turns into this wonderful person who even seems to like us," I said to Sue. "And then she leaves."

We sat there in the lounge for a minute or so, saying things back and forth like, do you think she's ok? Do you think the risers are high enough? Should we go kidnap the Dean? And then suddenly Sue's phone went off. She looked down and saw that it was a text message. Sue looked up and said, "It's from Lara. It says 'I miss you guys.'"

We walked back to the Guest House on Newberry Street. "Do you think we should go buy her a hair curler?" I asked. "I already did," Sue responded. "Why didn't she just go to UCSB?" I said. "They don't have to wear shoes at UCSB." "She wanted East Coast," said Sue. "Lara is a shoe person."

We took a shower and caught a cab to the Cheers bar, over on Beacon Hill. We'd never been there before, and we thought it might help "cheer" us up. "Hey look," I said. There it is." From the outside it looked just like Cheers. You walk down some stairs to the lower level and by golly you're in Cheers, except it was smaller and a lot louder and Ted Danson was a short black guy. We had a hamburger and beer. The place was OK as a novelty, but Sue and I were dazed and sad. Detroit was beating the Yankees on the big flat screen, so that was good. We looked in the gift shop and I bought a bar towel that said, "Cheers." We paid up and walked outside and: Wow!

When we looked up into the night sky we saw this big, bright, full and hopefully benevolent moon. It was a Boston night under a mysterious lunar influence. Sue took my arm. We decided to walk toward Beacon Hill to see the cobblestones and find John Kerry's house. "I think she was happy, don't you?" asked Sue. "Yeah. I think she was, but it's hard to tell. Lara doesn't show her feelings, especially if she's hurt or in need. She's a stoic." "I know. Remember those asthma attacks when she was little. She couldn't breathe. I mean no air, and yet she was so calm, so damn composed." We were getting sad again. Under the full moon, our hearts were heavy and I don't think Cheers or even John Kerry's house was going to be sufficient to lift this weight. We strolled over the cobblestones, arm-in-arm, and watched the moonlight reflect off the oddly curved surfaces, when suddenly the somber mood was broken by the sound of my cell phone. I flipped it open and put it to my ear. It was a voice message.

"I just had to call and tell you how amazing life is," said the message. It was Jessie. Jessie had arrived in Geneva, a few hours before. He was headed to a bicycle convention in Germany, but stopped over in Switzerland. He was on his bike, riding the entire circumference of Lake Geneva, so high on nature, endorphins and the inexhaustible fascination with being alive, that he couldn't resist picking up the phone and calling.

"Instead of flying to Munich," he said, "I took the train and laid over in Geneva. I'm riding all the way around Lake Geneva, over fifty miles. It's one of the most amazing rides I've ever taken. Remember, my friend, live big! Life's too short to be small."

He's done it again. From the other side of the planet but in complete concert with this milestone moment in our lives, Jessie just calls out of the blue and reminds us of . . . the mystery in charge of things. While listening to his message I was thinking, we're all angels in a way; each of us an angel to another.

But can you imagine me saying something like that out loud? No way. Sue would have pretended that it was really deep and everything, but inside she'd be going like, "huh? Are we in like a Unity church or something?" So I just handed her the phone and let her listen. She lifted her head and the moon lit up her face. She smiled and said, "He's like our angel."

I paused. My heart was in my throat. "You know the Large Hadron Collider is being built right there," I said, "hundreds of feet beneath the ground, right around the city of Geneva, where Jessie's riding his bike." We kept walking, looking up at the full moon and then down at the strange, ephemeral shadows that glowed so eerily on the cobblestones in front of John Kerry's house. "They're trying to recreate the conditions that existed at the beginning of the universe," I added with great emotion. "I think Jessie might be riding over the collider, at this very minute."

Home Alone

That was September. Back home the house was big, empty and quiet. For someone like Sue, there was only one way to fill the deep, unnerving void of Lara's absence: Redecorate!

Redo the family room. Get those travertine marble counters

we've always talked about for the kitchen. And of course file a claim for the water leak behind the refrigerator and use the insurance money to replace the worn out carpet with fake wood flooring.

As Lara began her college career, I too had my work cut out for me. I mean if there was a back story running behind the front story of Lara's departure, it was the existential question of whether to buy a new sofa or reupholster the old one that, in my view, ten years of professional sports and sitcom viewing had barely been broken in. For our younger readers this is an important point. You're probably saving to send your kids to college, but trust me: whatever you budget for tuition, room and board, add another 50% for the new furniture, paint and flooring that will be necessary the first semester of Freshman year.

By Fall of this year, of course, we were eating our hummus in quite a different world. Sue was sad, but busied herself with work, while I filled the void by complaining. Sue counted days til Thanksgiving break, mumbled things about Lara to Penny and took up sit-coms like *The Office, The New Adventures of Old Christine* and of course the entanglements taking place on Wisteria Lane. Instead of continually mourning Lara's absence, Sue stoically learned to text. I began a study of the life of William Shakespeare and discovered that the guy didn't actually exist. What a shock. Like me, he is a fictional character himself, invented for tourists by Prospero, the shaman from the well-known, but utterly misunderstood, play called "The Tempest." It's a complicated theory, which is good because my lengthy research has reduced the number of calls I was making to BU security, demanding they immediately place a 24-hour surveillance team on Lara's movements.

Lara herself embraced and was embraced by Boston. She learned the meaning of Winter, the quickest route across the Charles River to Harvard and how to dress for dinner. She mastered the subway system. She went to Red Sox games at Fenway Park (right across the street from her campus) which taught her the relationship between the word "fan" and the word "fanatic!" She navigated her way through the narrow, crowded corridors of dormitory life and overcame the confusing weirdness of roommates. Like Lizzy, for example.

Remember Lizzie. Beautiful Lizzie. When they decided to become roommates, it seemed like such a perfect match. She was not only bright, articulate and stylish, she was also a size 2, just like Lara. Being from Chicago, she helped Lara a lot with the concept of "warm coat." The two girls actually looked like sisters and it seemed like a beautiful relationship was underway. But gradually another person emerged, the one who installed the alarm system to protect their microwave oven from outsiders. The one who felt a need to put on rubber gloves before washing her face. The one who . . . Anyway: Lara and Lizzie are still good friends, but this year Lara upgraded to better housing and paired up with a strong, independent southern girl name Scarlett. She seemed perfect, too – kind, intelligent, gorgeous and so thoroughly self-aware — until she fell in love with this guy from Greece. He cheats. He lies. She loves him.

"We just have to go through this period," Scarlett explains to Lara about her relationship. "I'm sure he loves me." Lara stops trying to understand how this lovely, intelligent girl could abandon in such short order all of her self-respect, not to mention her rational mind, and for a guy named Agamemnon.

In a way, the sorority she joined this year became a true sanctuary. Delta-Gamma is a prestigious group of women on the BU campus. It has a long history with a powerful network of alumni that extends all across the country. Becoming a member of the executive board required a lot of old-fashioned lobbying. One didn't actually "campaign" for the position, one let others know of one's desire to serve, and this required months of what is known by professional lobbyists as "lunch." Now she has a leadership position and perhaps more important, a budget, which was right up there with those unknown foreign concepts like "winter coat."

But wait!

Sue just checked the Jet Blue Website and she did it! Her wheels are up and Lara is off the ground. The weather was so bad they couldn't take off with a full tank of gas, which means they don't have enough fuel to get them all the way to Long Beach. They have to stop and fill-up in Las Vegas; but who cares. Lara's in the air. Scheduled to land around 3:30 a.m. She'll be home for Christmas.

"Of splendour in the grass, of glory in the flower."

After a semester at college, all nine of the Ocho re-united here in Southern California during a break, and were spending days and nights talking philosophy. College had really ramped up their intellects and the conversation was on fire. "How's your college." "Good, how's yours?" "Mine's good, too." "Do you like your roommate?" "Yeah. She's cool. Same size as me. But she hooked up an alarm to the microwave, which was like the first sign of her disorder." "Yeah. I thought mine was cool, too. Then I found out she was from a really small state." "Yeah. You just never know who you're going to get."

This went on for a while when suddenly the girls realized they had forgotten to plan anything for New Years. In a sudden, middle-aged, psychotic break from reality, I stepped up and said something like, go ahead and have a party here at our house. Ten seconds later – through the use of an advanced communications technology called texting — thirty people had been invited, pizza and beer ordered and an array of illegal substances were making their way up from the border.

When I realized what I'd done, I panicked. Sue and I had nowhere to go and if we stayed at the house, Lara understood better than anyone that eventually, at some point in the evening, I would be unable to control my impulse to throw my arms into the air and, to all her friends, begin singing like, "There she goes just a walking down the street, singing doo waa diddy . . ." "You have to leave, Dad," she said.

But where?

That's how Sue and I ended up spending New Year's Eve at the Ritz Carlton Hotel, on the bluff, full-ocean view overlooking the deep Pacific. It was awesome. Plus, we were close enough to our house to hear it explode.

We were married at the Ritz Carlton like twenty years ago and it must have been a magical night because the only thing either Sue or I can recall is the exotic echo of the steel drums our dear friend Michael Rogers played for us, and then in the early morning hours seeing my Uncle Bob sound asleep in the flower beds. Remember the line from Wordsworth's famous poem *Intimations of Immortality from Recollections of Early Childhood?* The one that went, "Though nothing can bring back the hour / Of splendour in the grass, of glory in the flower". Ha! This is where the Romantic Poets got it all wrong. Wordsworth! Dude! You can totally bring it back. And we did. Me and Sue. The splendour of our wedding night in 1988 was back twenty years later, spectacular sunset; deep, abiding love. Better even than China.

After that, things just rolled along. We got up each morning. Fed the dog. Went to work. Called security at Boston University.

Then one day a strange thing happened. I think Lara was home for one of her breaks. She was reading in bed. I walked by her room scream-singing like, "I FEEEEEEL Good!" by James Brown. She went like "SHUT! UP!" and held up this big thick book in front of her face. "I've read fifty pages." I figured it was chick-lit; "Dead Men Don't Wear Gucci," or something. But when I looked closer I realized it wasn't "Blond Girls of Baghdad" or the scintillating, "Under the Sheets with Henry Kissinger;" No, it was "Portrait of a Lady" by Henry James, and it wasn't required reading. Lara was reading Henry James for fun.

I had to contain myself. "So, what did you think?" "It's very good. But the sentences!" And I thought uh oh; it's just too old fashioned for her. "Is it as bad as Jane Austin?" I probed. "No. Henry James wrote on the shoulders of Jane Austin," she replied, knowingly. "It's just amazing. I mean he could say, the girl got up and walked out of the room, but he takes like two chapters to get from the sofa to the door. Quite elegant." "Yes," I responded, a little like Obe Wan Kenobi. "A universe in a grain of sand. A lifetime on the way to the bedroom door."

With a totally unbiased paradigm, I can say that Lara's pretty remarkable in a lot of ways: in her insistence on happiness; her suspicion of "drama"; her refusal to give in to an attitude of male entitlement. And yet I swear she's still totally Kind. Funny. And so generous with our money.

"Did you know that DG was voted best sorority on campus?" she told me about a week after she'd arrived home. "What did you do your last night?" I asked. "Oh, we went to Harvard."

And she told us about these jaunts to the Harvard "Finals Houses." They're not fraternities. Harvard doesn't allow fraternities. Instead they call themselves, "Finals Houses" and they are VERY exclusive. The older girls in Lara's sorority have introduced Lara and the other younger girls to the social life at BU, especially to the social life that takes place in the Finals Houses across the river. You have to be on a list to get in. You have to know people. "They have just done so much for us," she said about the older girls. "What have they done?" asked Sue. "Introduced us to EVERYONE! Showed us EVERYTHING." She went on to tell us about how Dina was able to obtain two degrees in four years, "One in Public Relations and one in Poli Sci," she said. I sagaciously warned her about "over-achievers." "They really mess with the curve," I said. "But if she shares, that's good." Ignoring me completely she said, "She's going to New York. She's taking her LSAT. She's just amazing. And she showed us EVERYTHING." "Like what," I asked. "Like never walk into a party before eleven o'clock," she said. "And then walk straight to the bathroom."

One of the Finals Houses has a copy of Plato's "Republic" sitting right there on the deep dark mahogany book shelf. One of the sorority's big fund raisers this year, for the blind kids, is to steal "The Republic."

Heat Lightening

Most of '08 I was on the phone trying to raise money for tuition by finding someone to buy our kidneys, and Sue, after redecorating the curbs by our house, was on Expedia.com planning trips. In April, we combined a trip to visit Lara in Boston with a junket to Naples, Florida to see Sue's best friend, Lana.

I don't know how she does it, but whenever we travel, Sue always looks fresh as an English garden in the Spring and I always look like an industrial park. Here's an example: The two of us walk up to the check-in counter. The light from the sun outside seems to beam right through the windows of the terminal in such a way that it falls celestially over Sue's shoulders creating a brilliant golden halo, so illuminating her bright canary yellow jacket that a guy in a wheel chair behind us suddenly stood up and yelled, "I can walk! I can walk!" She has a carry-on that weighs the same as a box of popcorn and her purse floats on her arm like a soap bubble. I follow behind struggling with six heavy suitcases that contain all the equipment from my office, including my shelves, plus provisions recommended by Lewis and Clark. The two of us were standing at the counter and as I was wiping the sweat from my brow, the ticket agent said to Sue, "Flying alone today?"

Huh? Wait. Aren't I here? Isn't this me? This is how it always goes: Sue's all aglow with her deep blue saucer-sized eyes and I'm like . . . background.

But it doesn't stop there. The flight was so fully booked that we couldn't get seats together. "You can ask the cabin attendant to change your seats when you get into the aircraft," said the agent, adding for Sue's benefit, "but you don't have to." I was sitting next to this youngish looking guy and Sue was a few rows back. I leaned toward the guy and asked him if he would mind letting my wife sit next me. He said sure, and so I beckoned the cabin attendant. He walked back to Sue, who was healing the blind man sitting next to her. "You don't want to sit up there with him, do you?" he asked, squinting a bit from the glow.

Ha. Funny. He was joking of course, and it made me feel good that he recognized I was big enough to take a joke. Sue moved up, but just before she arrived at my row I suddenly realized we had a big problem. I looked up at the cabin attendant and then at the guy sitting next to me and said, "But if she moves up here, where will HE sit?" They all just looked at me like, Special Ed, right?

"Now that we're sitting together," I said to Sue, sounding quite a bit like Humphrey Bogart, "what do we say?" Before she could answer, however, I found myself doing a strange thing. I pulled up my collar and turned to a woman sitting on the other side of me. She was playing a hand of gin rummy with her own husband and seemed very content, until I intruded. She had seven playing cards in her hand and when I turned I could see them all. "We don't have anything to say," I repeated to the stranger. She turned to me and responded warmly, "It's just good to be close to each other on an airplane."

Then Sue leans over and adds, "He always puts his headphones on, and I can't tell him anything anyway." "Because you want to tell me about lamps," I reply, a little defensive. "And what do you want to talk about?" asks the lady as she lays down a seven of clubs. "Quantum Physics," I say. "The Large Hadron Collider. Palestine." "Lamps are better," she said the lady. I saw the winning move in her hand and found myself pulling the three of hearts out of her fingers and discarding it with a victorious flair I was certain the woman would appreciate. A broad smile fell across her husband's face as he picked up the card and said, "Gin."

I slid over closer to Sue, took her hand and we just went ahead and talked about Lara.

Naples, Florida was not unlike the glossier parts of Orange County, only more humid. There are lots of thick-leaved succulents; Big white flowers that require a steady diet of red meat; T-shirts with silhouettes of palm fronds and dolphins in different shades of pomegranate; and lots of things made out of green tea. While walking from Lana's house to the car, Sue discovered sweat, which was new for her. She called Lara in Boston to tell her about it, but Lara would not answer. We tried over and over again, but no answer. So, of course, I called BU security and asked them to send a team of forensic people to Lara's dorm. They found her in the laundry room. Apparently, she had been out to dinner with some sorority sisters, talking about how to steal Plato's *Republic,* and about their next charity event to free the world of facial blemishes. "We had a family dinner," she said (meaning her sorority sisters). "Wait a minute!" I objected. "I thought we were your family." "You've been replaced," she replied.

While Sue and Lana caught up on old times (When they were in college they had studied together in Salzburg, Austria, and have been close friends ever since.), I swam in the warm, aqua-marine waters of the Gulf and talked to myself about the Large Hadron Collider.

One hot tropical night we were walking Lana's dogs when off in the distance we saw a spectacular bolt of lightning crackle and branch across the twilit sky "Whoa! What the fuck was that?" I inquired. "Heat lightning, they call it," said Lana. When we got back to the house and turned on the television to get the forecast, a very serious weatherman was saying things like, "Don't mess with heat lightening. Don't hide under trees. Stay away from water. Don't even get a drink from the faucet because the lightening can run right up the plumbing and electrocute you right there at the sink." I looked up from the faucet at Sue, and she looked at me and we just laughed and laughed at that; then retired under the bed for the evening.

Boston of course is a lot colder than Naples and I was glad I brought the three suitcases with mittens. Once we had arrived at the little Bed and Breakfast on Newbury Street we called Lara and made arrangements to meet her at the quaint café located down the street, inside the Trident Bookstore. Sue made sure we were there two hours early; so we had a lot of time to adjust to Bostonian ways. The thing I like most about Boston is taking off my coat and putting it over the back of the chair. Growing up in Southern California, we never had an opportunity to do that. We'd maybe slip our sandals off, or roll up the sleeves of our t-shirt, but no one that I knew ever had a jacket to take off. So whenever we arrived at a place like the Trident Bookstore I would always help Sue off with her coat and then, like a cool character from some really neat independent foreign film, I'd like take off my jacket and with great panache, position it over the back of my chair.

When Lara finally walked into the café, it was as if Sue had been struck by heat lightning: first she was stunned with delight. Then tears of joy ran down her cheeks and into her herbal tea. I felt the same way, but again, Sue gets away with expressions of emotion for which I risk embarrassment and sometimes even arrest. Lara does look beautiful; just luminous, like a Christmas display window at Bergdorf's and Goodman's. She has not only inherited her mother's core, which is like the center of the sun, but has also acquired a studied sartorial sense that appears "thrown-together," but is not the least bit careless. Lara has not only mastered the concepts of "winter coat," "neurotic roommate," and "lunch" this year, she has also added a cool element of style.

As I helped her off with her coat and give her a big hug, I felt again the mystery of life flowing through me, culminating as always in a profound sense of complete and utter confusion; which I countered by faking an assertive, "Lara! You're here!"

For a while, the conversation pertained to Democratic primaries and the happenings at school. Like most progressive people who were old enough to have witnessed the sixties evolve from youthful idealism into a fetid stool of license and hypocrisy, I was for Hillary Clinton. "Idealism without experience leads to . . . unwanted children," I said. I felt the change we wanted in the country cried out for intelligence and hardcore political savvy, and of course it was way past time for a president who knew how to cook and clean. Sue was for Hillary, too. Lara was weighing the virtues of Edwards and Obama, but was leaning toward Obama. She had seen all three of them in person when they came to Boston and spoke at the Commons. As she explained with surprising erudition and nuance that I was too old to really understand anything that happened in the world after the cancellation of *The Mod Squad*, I noticed that she was talking a little funny. I felt her throat. Her tonsils were the size of grapefruits. I felt her head and it was burning up. "Lara, honey! You're sick," I said. "Yeah," she said. "I have a sore throat."

So that summer, (last summer) Lara spent three weeks here slurping down sherbet smoothies, reading the collected works of Henry James and recovering from her tonsillectomy. Sue and I sold the tonsils for a pretty good price and used the money to go to Salzburg, Austria. The group she had studied with in Austria has remained very close during the subsequent four decades and they organized a reunion in Mozart's hometown to celebrate their new hips and knees.

But wait!

The doorbell just rang. I think it's Amanda and Taylor.

When you were a sophomore in college how close were you with the people in your third-grade class? I know. Me, too. No one. And yet Taylor and Amanda drove all the way over here just to decorate Lara's room before she got home. Amanda is Lara's Secret "Ocho" Santa. She brought her a pendant and homemade fudge as a gift. Lara loves homemade fudge, as long as it's made with cocoa from her favorite village in the Bolivian Andes. They walked right upstairs and hung the welcome home and Merry Christmas banner in her room, and then came down and were gracious enough to spend some time talking to me and Sue.

I'm one of the millions upon millions of American guys who grew up in lowered, metal-flaked automobiles thinking they would never (ever) reach the age of thirty. Yet here I am, like weeks beyond that; And so much has happened? That's why it's still a little unreal to be sitting on our stairway with Amanda and Taylor, both bright, stylish and witty coeds who I remember as fourth-graders at Lara's birthday party. Taylor was always the clever instigator, like that night they made me drive them round the neighborhood at three in the morning to toilet paper the homes of guys they were pretending not to like. (I was the only one that got busted for that night.) Now she's a sophisticated journalism major at UCSB who spent last summer in Oxford, England learning how to make the "t" sound when saying the word "butter," "better" and "Betty." Amanda is a journalism major, too, at Cal State San Luis Obispo (SLO). She's more understated than Taylor, but she has a twisted wisdom beyond her years and has a sense of humor and oblique take on existence that is thoroughly original. Sue and I are on the steps asking them the usual questions, how do you like college? What are your plans? Can I have some of that fudge?

"I loved Oxford," said Taylor. (See? That's what I mean. Back when I was just a kid, lying in the grease beneath my metal-flaked 1954 Chevrolet, using a blow-torch to heat the front coil springs so the car would drop lower to the ground, I never thought in a million years that anyone would ever say to me, "I loved Oxford.")

"The classes were awesome," she continued. "I even had one called 'Espionage and the Media' which reminded me of you.
"Yeah," I said. "But you know I can't talk about that."

I think Sue and I have always been a bit of a mystery for Lara's friends. As you probably know, while working in Iran during the Islamic Revolution, I found it necessary to become a Muslim cleric. Converting to Islam enabled me to smuggle money and secret documents, not to mention my girlfriend and her young son, out of the country. At about the same time (around 1979), ten years before I had even met her, Sue was converting to the Jewish religion (true story), "because I found it to be so life affirming," she said. So technically, Lara is of the Jewish/Muslim persuasion which, as I have pointed out in previous Christmas letters, makes her an original; and perhaps destined to lead the two antagonistic groups out of the warring desert and into the promised land, which several prophets have predicted will be named "Bloomingdalia."

Taylor, Amanda and the other Girls of Ocho, plus several very suspicious parents, have always been a little "uncertain" about my history. "You never go to work," explained Amanda. "And you get all those strange deliveries to your house," said Taylor. "And then you lived in all those illegal countries." "Yeah, Yeah," I said. "It was a matter of . . . circumstances." I pulled up my collar around my neck and squinted my eyes so I looked quite a bit like Clint Eastwood. "Just gimme that small piece of fudge and I'll tell you what really happened."

Primaries in the Alps

Sue checked the Jet Blue website for an update on Lara's flight and it looked like it was going to land in Long Beach at three in the morning. It's beginning to feel like Christmas. I guess I should wind this up. In all seriousness, the last few months have been difficult, and not just for Hillary Clinton.

We watched her concede to Obama on a small television screen in a tiny room in a pension not far from the train station in Salzburg. Nestled in the northern foothills of the Austrian Alps, where Einstein attended his first physics convention and

MARK MENDIZZA

Mozart wrote the original version of "I Feel Good!", Salzburg is like a second home for Sue. She lived there during the 1970s while pretending to study the works of Hugo von Hofmannsthal. She's been back many times, and whenever she comes within range of the Festung, the Medieval fortress on top of one of the many hills that surround the city, her pulse increases and she starts muttering things like "Bier und Schnitzel, bitte" and "Ich bin ein Salzburger!" I mean almost any location more than fifty miles away from the tedium our house is like a spiritual Red Bull for Sue, but Salzburg is an elixir that goes beyond even the magic of caffeine and dense concentrations of amino acids, especially when Die Gruppe (Bill, Dallas, Steve, Lana and Wunderbear) is there.

Die Gruppe is basically Sue's version of the Ocho, ten or so people who so tightly bonded during their foreign studies that they deemed the rich, besotted experience not just worth preserving year after year, stein after amber stein, but actually worth re-enacting it.

Bill tells everyone that he heads up the graduate program in the business school at Seattle University. That prestigious MBA program seems to consist of making mandatory trips to Tuscany each year to pay homage to Luca Pacioli, the 15th century creator of modern double-entry bookkeeping. Once you have completed the required number of toasts to Pacioli, and purchased the requisite round of drinks, Bill presents you with a Master's degree, right there in the bar. So far no one at the school seems to have heard of him.

Dallas is a practicing Sufi. Apparently, Sufism is something you have to practice your whole life, or until you can say, "Red Leather Yellow Leather" three times real fast. Sufism too requires a substantial amount of drinking, preferably abroad, away from the children in the ashram. Thus, Dallas's spiritual pilgrimage to Salzburg. The group likes to test his mystical powers by sneaking off to little known bars in the city without telling Dallas when or where they're going; then see how many drinks it takes before he discovers their whereabouts. The trippy thing about Dallas is he's usually sitting there at the bar, waiting for them when they arrive.

Steve is an accountant who used to work for the IRS, specializing in sending people like me to jail. Then he quit to join a big firm in the private sector and two weeks later he was so rich he bought the state in which he lives; Maryland I think. He is a worldly guy, now; with his own vineyards, record label and start-up company specializing in space exploration vehicles equipped with kegs that are cooled by keeping them outside the space capsule during inter-galactic flights. With all of his wealth, however, Steve has never found anything more amusing than putting on his lederhosen and favorite zither CD, and drinking with his old friends from Salzburg.

Lana is kind of an heiress, from an old aristocratic family that made its fortune in peanut butter and jelly. She travels from one of her many estates to another during the off-season — which is whenever Die Gruppe is not together drinking — saving stray animals and recalculating, over and over again, the year people say she was born.

Lana and Sue are more like sisters than friends; almost twins. We have photos of them when they were young girls living in Cleveland, Ohio. One shows them back in the 70's standing in front of the TWA DC 1 that was to transport them to Salzburg. Each is dressed in a proper wool knit skirt with well-regulated hems just below the knees, a prim three-button jacket, and both were clutching a little pocket book in virginal hands protected from the corrupt reality of the outside world by a pair of neat white gloves. "Avon ladies," said Wunderbear.

Like the Ocho, Die Gruppe is a random, self-organizing entity, but Wunderbear might be thought of as a leader, if only because of the long crimson robes and platter-sized gold medallion he is authorized to wear. A Washington lobbyist by profession, Wunderbear's eternal passion has always been saying the words, Pinot Grigio. So he became a wine connoisseur. He researched the most prestigious wine institutes in the world and when he found one in France that issued long red robes he signed right up. Today Wunderbear is a master. He can sniff a glass of wine and not only give you the GPS coordinates of the vineyard, but also name all the grandchildren of the peasant who picked the grapes. Wunderbear retired recently in order to spend more time with his favorite menus. After lobbying his wife for airfare, he made the trip to Salzburg and joined Die Gruppe in the little pension where Sue, me, Bill, Dallas, Lana and Steve sat around a little table drinking toasts to von Hofmannsthal and the weird defeat of Hillary Clinton.

But Salzburg wasn't at all the quiet Alpine hamlet that Die Gruppe had so fondly remembered. Instead of the sherry-sipping Baroquies that usually frequent the Residenzplatz, the Mozartplatz and the new Budweisserplatz, the city was teeming with rowdy European soccer fans from all over the continent. "Our timing couldn't have been worse," said Bill, who liked to wander the quiet Platzes , humming Die Zauberflaute and recruiting graduate students. "The Residenzplatz has a big rock "n" roll stage and there are drunken Swedes in the fountain." Without informing anyone in Die Gruppe, Austria and Switzerland chose to host Soccer 08, the European championship soccer tournament held every four years between the years when the World Cup is held. (Apparently this was the only way to make sure that every two years the Swedes have reasons to jump into the fountains.) Teams and fans from as far off as Europe converged on the city of Salzburg at the same time as Die Gruppe arrived. In fact, Sue and I were sharing a room with the Bosnian team.

I wish I could tell you everything about the journey to Salzburg, but alas, like Isabel Archer's walk from the sofa to the doorway, it would take many hundreds of pages to describe. Instead, I'll just point out the key cultural things that distinguish Austrian culture from our own. For one: they eat bologna for breakfast. I don't know where that came from. Scholars are doing paradigms on the subject, but so far no one really knows why there are so many cold cuts on an Austrian breakfast buffet. Another cultural thing you probably don't know about is Gulaschsuppe. Most of you when you think of Austria think of Vienna, Johann Strauss and the waltz. Some may think about Loden Wool and Sacher Torts. And I know one sick friend who still thinks about Sigmund Freud's theory of infant sexuality. But I don't think anyone thinks about gulaschsuppe.

But gulasch is big. And it makes sense. Austria is bordered on the east by the Czech Republic, Slovakia, Hungary and other nations with a rich goulash history. Some have even gone to war over it. So just leave it to Wunderbear to take us on his famous gulaschsuppe tour of Salzburg.

Actually, I would just call it a walk. But Wunderbear has a way of turning a walk (or just standing around) into something . . . well, intoxicating. The way it goes is you all get together and start strolling through the ancient city, looking at the cool

Baroque architecture, comparing the Austrian cobblestones to the ones in front of John Kerry's house, seeing if you can guess the nationality of the guy who just puked in the fountain. You stroll along the river. You start to climb the circuitous pathways up toward the Festung, when suddenly Wunderbear utters the word, "Hydrate!"

Everyone stops. "It's been quite a hike so far," he pants, even though it's only been a few hundred feet. "We have to hydrate."

We enter a little tavern where we arrange our seating according to Bill's "small-table" school of daytime drinking. "Small tables bring people closer together," he says, as we scrape our little bent-wood chairs across the floor toward a café table the size of a schilling. "It's a technique I use in my classes to encourage intimacy and candor." "But we've known each other for forty years," complains Dallas, while also struggling to practice his Sufism. "We need room for steins."

The waiter approaches the table and we all look toward Wunderbear. "Ein bier und gulaschsuppe, bitte," he says. This seems a little strange to me because it's only been ten minutes since our breakfast bologna. But no one knows food and drink better than Wunderbear, and so we all order gulaschsuppe and bier. Feeling quite intimate around the tiny table, we sip, slurp and reveal our inner most secrets.

Then we walked out to the cobble-stoned streets and continued our tour. We cruised by the Abbey where Julie Andrews was excommunicated. We stopped for a moment on the site were Herbert von Karajan decided to change his first name to Jim. We listened to the cathedral bells echoing throughout the city, followed by, "Need to hydrate!"

Another tavern. More bier. And a second gulaschsuppe.

By mid-day we were thoroughly intoxicated by the sites and charm of Salzburg. We had sampled gulaschsuppe from sixteen locations throughout the city. Our cheeks were rosy as an Austrian hausfrau. The rims of our mouths a uniform blood-red from the on the gulashsuppe. During our intimate small-table talks I found an opportunity to explain how the theory of quantum mechanics (which transcends not only time and causality, but also addition and subtraction) made it possible for Albert Einstein to author King Lear and the other plays attributed to Shakespeare. We had no secrets.

And yet, the journey was not over. We were being seated yet again at a tiny little table on the outdoor terrace of a place called Stiegl Brau, which is Salzburg's premier pilsner brewery (founded in 1492, almost a hundred years after the founding of the Forbidden City), known the world over not only for its excellent Stiegl, but also for its brau. The sun was warm. The breeze cool. We had a beautiful view of the Festung looming mysteriously on the white limestone hill above us and of the meandering river, the Baroque steeples and ten thousand shit-faced European soccer fans below, all of who were singing their individual national anthems.

"Gulaschsuppe!" I blurted out in perfect German, as I fell back into my chair. "Ein und zwanzig Stiegl, Sie vous plait, und gulaschsuppe fur alles!"

By this time Die Gruppe had begun to see through much of my charm. After all, this was THEIR reunion and the gulaschsuppe und bier had paved the way toward a deep and inaccurate nostalgia, reminiscing about their younger days in Salzburg before their butts got really big. They laughed fondly at the quirkiness of their old professors. They recalled with affection the neighborhood where they had lived together in small apartments. Lana brought out some old postcards that she had sent to her parents while she and Sue were studying at the University. They had so much fun passing them around and reading the cute little notes Lana had written as a student.

> Hi Dad,
> Have to go to class now.
> Could you wire a little extra money.
> Love you. Lana

> Gruss Gott!
> Can't believe we've been here six years!
> Definitely deciding on a major this semester.
> Running out of money, though!
> Love, Lana

> Dear Dad,
> Greetings from Stiegl Brau,
> Finally getting focused!
> The title of my senior thesis is, "Dialects of the Austrian Biergarten 1900 - Today."
> Might do MBA on Luca Pacioli.
> Need that money.
> Prost!, Lana.

Probably the most striking thing that occurred to me during the gulaschsuppe tour and the other little side trips was seeing how animated, I might even say transformed, Sue became while in the company of her old friends. When she's with me she's so afraid of the way I drive or of what I might do or say in public that I think it prevents her from being herself. But with Lana and Steve and Dallas there to help talk to the police, I think Sue felt much less inhibited. She was making jokes and laughing so hard that she cried, and someone said that for a brief moment they thought they saw a wrinkle form. It was more than just the wine and beer. It was being in Austria. It was the magical atmosphere of Salzburg. She just came to life.

I remember the night we went to the cave bar. I don't recall the name of this place, but it was a dark, moody little pub that had literally been carved out of the side of the mountain, so the walls were like, rock. Once again, we were sitting around a small table celebrating life and discussing our tastes in classical music. Bill had brought a female friend, an Englishwoman who was living in Italy and who helped him organize the mandatory trips to the birthplace of Luca Pacioli. An Englishwoman, just by making her "t" sounds, always tends to raise the level of discourse among Americans, and Rohaise did so for Die Gruppe. "I only like classical music composed before Mozart," she eloquated. And of course we're all like nodding, uh-huh; comparing it to only liking stuff before Vic Damone. "I like bits of others, but it's the music of Monteverdi that I really like." Uh-huh. Yeah. I can understand that. And we're going like, Monteverdi?

Wunderbear thought Monteverdi was a bulk wine. Lana said she'd named one of her stray dogs Monty. And I finally had to step in and explain that Monteverdi was the neighborhood in East L.A. where Hugo Chavez was born.

As in any deep, erudite discussion of the classics, the subject of ABBA came up. You may recall from an earlier Christmas Letter, we became closet ABBA lovers back when we took Lara and her friends to see the West Coast premiere of "Mama Mia". I can still remember that night because I was adamant about not going into the theater and listening to that adolescent music from the 80s. "I'll just sit in the car and think about the Higgs Particle," I said. "You guys go ahead." But as usual, Sue bought me a ticket and I've been listening to "Dancing Girl" ever since.

And guess what? The English woman popped up with, "I've been listening to ABBA since I was four years old, ever since I used to drive around with my mother." That was a relief. This sophisticated woman adored ABBA. And then Bill said, "I've never heard ABBA." And we're like huh? "I had several chances to see Mama Mia," he continued. "I was in London looking for something to do and I saw this show "Mama Mia", but I thought it was about the Italian Mafia."

So we all started saying how great ABBA was. And his English friend told us how every milestone in her youth was marked by an ABBA tune and that without those songs she wouldn't know who she was. And we're going like, BILL! You've never heard an ABBA song? And he said, and these are his exact words, "I'm always listening to music, but never in an era that corresponds to my lifetime." And once again, like how many times is this going to happen, we're going like, huh?

So I got up and walked over to the bartender and asked him in perfect Austrian German, "Haben Sie ABBA, bitte? "Are you kidding," he said. "Was Hitler a Schniklegruber?" And he put on a CD with all kinds of ABBA music.

First Sue started tapping her foot on the ground. Then kind of waving back and forth to the rhythm. And then she just blurted out, "How can you all just sit here!" Which I took as some kind philosophical question.

Sue got up and began to dance in the middle of the cave bar. Lit by the glow from the foot-high glasses of beer that were like torches inside the dark; it was a scene from a dream. Not just that she was dancing, but that she was dancing like a really good dancer; extraordinary rhythm and erotic moves. Everyone turned around in their chairs and just stared at her, as amazed as I was. Stunned, really. Too stunned, of course, to get up and dance with her, which would have been the gentlemanly thing to do. But Sue didn't care. Sue wasn't Sue anymore. She'd been transported. She was the dancing girl.

Mom's Sick

Not long after we got home, Sue's mom was diagnosed with pancreatic cancer and given at most a few months to live.

Sue collapsed, even though it seemed time for her mother to move on. She was over ninety-five years old. She'd suffered physically. Her awareness and memory and language had deteriorated to the point where she began to sound like me. And during the brief flashes when she seemed in possession of herself she expressed her own desire to "die." But the information, when it comes, is still like a body blow; no: like a flurry, like a combination of blows to the ribs, the solar plexus, the head and heart.

The sadness came over Sue in waves of memory; about her mother's suffering and her long struggle with what might be called a normal socialization. Her mom had been a little awkward and isolated from other people. Sue and then Lara had become her mother's sole source of happiness and satisfaction, and there was a sadness in that, not to mention an enormous burden for an only child. Sue felt the primal sadness that comes from losing the only person left in her immediate family, and sadder still I think that her mother was leaving the world without having fully touched so many of its joys. "I just feel so alone," she said once. "Lara doesn't call. You're gone all the time. I just feel so alone." In all the time I have known her, these are words that had never left her lips.

I sat with her on the sofa and held her and said, "But I bought you that cool tool belt last Christmas. That's something isn't it?"

I held her for a while as she sobbed in my arms. "I think it's premature, sweetheart. Nothing's actually happened yet. She's eating. She's drinking. She's okay right now. I'll call Doctor Cohen. I'll find out how all this works. Let's take it one day at a time, okay?" She caught her breathe. Relaxed a little. "I really want a new bed," she said. "We need to get a king-sized bed."

I remember sitting in my car outside the office of one of the graphic artists that works for me. I had called Dr. Cohen. After listening to Sue tell me about her conversation with him, I wanted to try and clear up some things in my own mind: how certain is he about the diagnosis? How does a disease like this shake out? What's the general wisdom about whether we should tell Sue's mom that she is dying?

A large mass at the front of the pancreas, creating pressure on the bile duct. Dr. Cohen had been in this business for a long time and he knew what he was talking about. I know all about the bile duct. My Dad died of a cancerous bile duct. My friend Peggy is struggling with a mass on her pancreas that has blocked her bile duct. It's like jaundice all over the place. "I do this every day," Dr. Cohen said. "And it was still surreal watching my father die. Completely unreal. And I live with the dying every day." That rang true. The sensation that overcomes one while watching another person pass is probably the starkest event one will ever face, and yet totally unreal.

Sue and I sat across a round table from the hospice people that had come to consult with us. A woman named Debbie talked and talked about the program, all the things that hospice was and wasn't; all the things they would do for Edna, much of which had to do with morphine. I finally had to cut her off and say, "Can we meet the nurse? We want to get to know the person who will be caring for Edna." "Of course you can meet her," said Debbie. "Well, actually," I said, "we want more than that. We want to like her." Debbie paused. "The truth is, if they're in hospice care, they are going to be pretty nice. There aren't too many meanies who go into this kind of work." And I thought to myself, "Good point."

Sue spent time with her mother every day, visiting with her and saying her good-byes. Sometimes her mother knew who Sue was and at others she didn't; her memories just seemed to leap incoherently from one era of her life to another; so rapid and sporadically that no one understood their relationship to her mother's life, not even her mother. It was difficult for Sue, not to be recognized. More than difficult: it was at a very deep level, the most tragic thing that can occur between a mother and daughter. But then there were other times; these sudden, pristine moments when Edna would just look up and say something like, "Oh it feels so good to be alive!" And she would turn to Sue and say, "And to have you here with me, my beautiful daughter."

The hard part was the ache and pain that Sue had to suffer, day in and day out as the process inched along. Only children bare this burden in multiples; unable to hand off the responsibility to a brother or sister or even an aunt or uncle or ... Anyone.

Sue was on her own, strong as Everest, but in her strength, she wept and grieved. That is the hard part, that and still having to put up with me and my stubborn belief that life is more than a great suffering; that it is also a great "complaining."

One night instead of watching Anderson Cooper, Sue and I lit a candle, laid down in the den and listened to a recorded talk by the late Elizabeth Kubler-Ross. She spoke with certainty about the dying experience and the afterlife. "There ARE angels. There are guides. They ARE here, now. They will be there after you die." Sue and I had met Kubler-Ross many years ago and had remembered how charismatic she was, and how much sense she made, even though everything she said was logically beyond the pale. She possessed what seemed an innate credibility that rose up out of her molten life experience like a geyser in Yellowstone, and you just "believed" what she said. Her work in Europe with holocaust victims, in Chicago with dying children, and her pioneer hospice work; It was almost quaint to hear her talk about cosmic consciousness because it sounded so sixtyish, but we were certain her remarks derived from a vivid, unequivocal personal experience. Guardian angels. Spiritual guides. A realm of unconditional love. And the need to recognize and eliminate "our little Hitlers." It sounded almost Medieval, but while Sue and I laid there with our eyes closed – she on the love seat with her feet up on the armrest and me on the floor with my meditation pillow under my head — listening to Kubla-Ross speak in that adorable Swiss accent about the stark reality of another, more perfect world, it affected us. It did something more than just console us about the experience her mother was going through, it hearkened to something deeper, reminding us of things we vaguely believe; drew them forward and made more visible and audible; something about our own guides, our own angels. Our souls.

In a nutshell she said the only question you are going to be asked after you die and move on to the Promised Land is "How many people have you helped? How much service have you provided?" We both agreed that her mom's history of nursing should get her ticket punched, and that it would be a good idea to maybe look for some volunteer work myself.

Sometimes I would go over and visit with Edna myself. It was difficult, first because she was not conscious and second because the whole environment of extreme age and decline was foreign, and frankly unnerving to me. Since we couldn't interact normally, I would just spend time talking to her, mostly about her own life, recalling for her the time, sixty years or so ago, when as a young woman just off her nursing shift in Cleveland, she drove to a downtown auditorium to see a new Italian crooner named Frank Sinatra. Even at ninety-five years old, she had always swooned a little while recalling that night. Then I sat down and read out loud: Wordworth's "Intimations of Immortality": "Though inland far we be, / Our Souls have sight of that immortal sea . . . / And see the Children sport upon the shore, / And hear the mighty waters rolling evermore."

I'd end my visit by singing. I know it sounds a little weird, but I felt I had to break through the dark walls that tend to surround the dying, and the only way I could think of to do that was to sing "Sunrise-Sunset", from Fiddler. And then that Tony Bennett song, "Because of You." Ending the set with, "When somebody loves you / It's no good until they love you / Alllll the way . . ." While I was singing, one of the other residents in the room next door, a large woman over three hundred pounds, had slipped into a fit of crazed dementia and was cursing the caregivers. "Fuck you! Fuck you, you sonofabitch," she was yelling. "You can't do this to me!" It was as if the outside world was trying to encroach on the moment. But I had gotten used to the devil in things, not just in the assisted-care facility, but in all things. I have found the devil generally hates singing, especially mine. So I gently closed the door to the room and continued with "All the way . . .," pretty certain that the spirit was getting through, helping clear a pathway from our inland realm to the mighty waters rolling evermore.

Lara was the last to see her before she passed. We had planned to fly out to Boston and spend Thanksgiving with her on the East Coast, but we cancelled and she came home instead. It was as if her grandmother had waited for her, postponed her departure until she could have just one more fleeting glimpse of Lara. Which she did. Lara staid with her for a while, playing some music and just trying to keep her company, and then she came home and we had a little birthday party for Lara, just the three of us.

It was around nine o'clock at night. I was in my robe, getting ready to lie down on the newly upholstered sofa and watch "Rio Grande", a movie starring John Wayne and Maureen O'Hara, directed by John Ford. Sue was in bed. Lara was upstairs texting to her network. The vast roseate landscapes of the West filled the screen and seemed to tell a story all its own, just the camera pans of the sculpted, stratified mesas cut through by a few hundred million years of rushing rivers. It was an epic tale told in geological time that made the machismo of the U.S. Cavalry galloping around and hollering out things like, "Corporeal! Sound reveille" and "Whoaa!" seem quaint, even ridiculous. John Wayne was sporting a big wing-tipped mustache. The phone rang. It was my cell, and by the time I got upstairs to retrieve it, it had stopped ringing. Then Sue's cell began to ring. I bounced back down to the family room where it was vibrating like a dying animal on the brown English breakfast table. Arthur. Arthur from assisted living. Uh-oh. "I think Edna has passed," he said in his dignified if slightly awkward accent. I swear it felt like what it felt like when Sue started having her contractions: here we go. Irreversible . . .

Even after all Sue had gone through — I mean the process had been so arduous and relentless — when I walked upstairs and told her that her mom had passed, it was like the earth had stopped for a moment its orbit around the sun; everything just stopped.

"When?," she asked. "Was anyone there? Was Arthur there? Was she alone?" A suppressed . . . panic; a feeling as delirious as Hamlet's, who knew all too well what could not be comprehended in this world. "He was with her," I said. "He said he just walked out to the garage for a moment and when he returned she had stopped breathing." We're in our pajamas. It's night time. It's dark. This is a damned incorrigible thing: this raging, humbling undeceiver. "The nurse from hospice was there. She said there was really no need to go down and see her. It was all pretty routine at this point."

To me, this seemed as odd and frankly as cold as a tax audit. Sue looked like she'd been stabbed. This can't be right. But what do I know. We know nothing of the particulars. All we know is the goddamn theory of it, the idea of passing: that's it. "She said they would call the coroner and get a number, and then they would call the mortuary and they would come and pick her up and then we could talk to them in the morning."

"What about her gold dress?" Sue asked. "I placed her gold dress there on the barrel table. Will they put her in the dress? It was the dress she bought when we made the decision that she should move from Ohio to California. It was the most expensive dress she ever bought."

"You know, I don't know. I've never done this before," I said."

"Call Diane." She said.

"It was an important catharsis for me," Diane said about being with her own mother when she had passed. "Just seeing her, seeing the body there made it all much more real, because that wasn't my mother. My mother had been released from that body. She was finally free, and being there, seeing it brought that home to me, made it concrete. That she was finally free. It's something I really needed."

Diane is another of our many angels.

The rains had begun to fall hard. As Sue, Lara and I drove together down to the assisted living house, it poured down harder and harder. Sue had been waiting for a psychic signal that her mother had died. She is so intuitive; almost psychic I'd say. But she did not receive that profound impulse, that signal that she had heard about from other women and that she halfway expected. It didn't seem to come. She had been asleep.

Secretly, I was very suspicious of women who had reported such things. I believed Elizabeth Kublar-Ross, but was skeptical about stories like, I knew the moment my mother passed away, even though I was in Lawndale and she was in like Galveston. But I don't express any skepticism. I was strictly a believer. "You know what? This rain is the sign. The rain began the moment she passed. She went up there and goddamn shook up the heavens, you know. It is very auspicious: it is life giving. It is a promise." And I believed what I was saying.

We walked into her room. The earth had yet to move. It was utterly still, and Sue's mom was on her back, dressed in the lovely yellow dress that Arthur had so kindly, so reverently helped with. She was no longer there. Or rather, she was no longer on the bed. Diane was right about that. The spirit had risen.

Sue wept. She slipped to the floor at the foot of the bed and for a while held her mother's hand. Lara, with a strength so profound and that I so welcomed, lowered herself to her mother's side and held her in her arms, and the two wept together. I sat slightly off to the side, trying to know this thing, waiting for the earth to move again, and playing big band music and Frank Sinatra songs on the little player we had bought to help comfort her mom. I kept the volume low.

Garlic Shrimp

"The air. The air. Do you feel the air?" said Sue. We were driving our little rented white car on the island of Oahu, heading to the North Shore where we had booked a few nights to try and recover from the last few ... you know: decades. It had been a week since we held the service for Sue's mom in our back yard. I don't know if you'd call it a funeral, but we had a little service, just a few of Sue's close friends from the college, Jimmy and Diane from down the street, Lara, my sister and brother and Penny. Jimmy and Diane sang the "Lord's Prayer" and "Amazing Grace." What genuine artists they are, such angels they have been to us. Marsha, my sister, is a minister and she presided in the most gracious and sensitive way. The mountains in the background lent their eternal beauty to the event. It was perfect. We bid our good byes and could feel her Mom spiraling up to the eternal everywhere and beyond, arm-in-arm with a cadre of white winged angels and sober celestial guides. We rolled down the windows of the little car and felt the moist tropical air that was so fertile and nurturing that big fragrant plumeria blossoms just bloomed spontaneously in the air around us. It was so fresh. The earth was back in orbit.

And I have to say, we have some good karma. Remember when we were in Salzburg and just coincidentally all the soccer teams from the European continent happened to be there, too; competing to see how many of each team could fit at one time into the fountain outside of Mozart's house? Well, when we arrived at the North Shore guess what? Not more Swedes; but a lot of Surfers.

It was the end of the season for world-class surfing competitions. The North Shore waves were huge, especially at Pipeline, and the day we arrived they announced the Billabong Pipeline Masters was about to convene. The greatest surfers on earth were gathering to face the Pipeline. Whoa! Where's my board? While driving I was, as usual, on the phone to Lara in Boston, where she had resumed her leadership responsibilities, which included reviving the entire U.S. economy with nothing more than my American Express Gold card. She had just finished her first six-hour executive planning session, which had been held in the apartment of one her sisters. "She's from Oahu," Lara said, loudly. "She's so proud of being born in the same place where Obama grew up." "Tell her your Mom and dad are on the way to the North Shore," I said. "Tell her the Pipeline Masters is taking place. Ask her where I can get a board."

We spent several days and nights in the warm embrace of sea and sky. The boisterous surf scrubbed away dead skin, the receding tide rinsed away the residue; the warm tropical air blew memory itself out to sea and left us in a pure, seemingly endless present. I swam in the cove and Sue took long invigorating walks along the shore. We could actually feel the healing taking place, like one of those cinematic special effects in which the gaping mortal wound suddenly sutures back together on its own, without scar or any other sign of injury. We were whole again. If only the world itself, the world of suffering and complaint, could just swim for a while in tropical waters, then soak in the Jacuzzi as Sue and I did; eat hamburgers, drink cold draft beer together, and watch the sun set, listen to the stars come out. How could we then not reach agreement?

I was dazed, of course. There was so much activity going on around me, and yet it occurred within this warm amniotic environment that felt so protected and secure and nourishing that being psychotic was actually kind of comforting. The acrobatic surfers were out there finding their way through the turbulent forces of nature, riding superbly formed waves, proud of their very existence. The new mother in her miniscule bikini, holding her child in her arms and still feeling sexual toward her naked husband who walked up and put his arms around them both. The crowd of resort people holding their cell phones up in the air and pointing them toward the setting sun, trying to capture the image and the ephemeral atmosphere it had created in this mothering place; wanting so badly to send it instantly to friends and family back home. Everyone in shorts and sandals sipping smoothies, draft beers in plastic cups and the killer ice teas they make with vodkas from countries one has never heard of. It all felt so relaxed and dreamy, vivid yet other-worldly. And for us, it was the aftermath: the irresistible oceanic surge that swells up like the waves in the sea and breaks eternally on our shore with the furious sound of an unequivocal promise: there will be more and more and again more.

When I told Jessie we were going to the North Shore of Oahu, he only had one thing to say: garlic shrimp!

"You've got to try the garlic shrimp," he said. "Only on the North Shore of Oahu, and only from the trucks parked on the side of the road."

So Sue and I set out to find the truck on the side of the road that sold the garlic shrimp. The roads curved inland and out, and at every turn we witnessed a beautiful cove with a beach that looked like it had been painted into the landscape. We cruised north and it was beautiful, and then a little bit west where it was beautiful, and suddenly we saw a big old beat-up truck on the side of the road. It was painted bright yellow with big red letters written in the primitive hand of a child or a non-native speaker of the language. It read, "Fumi's Garlic Shrimp."

We quickly pulled into the little gravel lot and parked. Behind the truck was a large canopy that protected about eight redwood picnic tables from the tropical sun. It was a warm, balmy day. The soul-nourishing trade winds caressed us and the clouds were passing by in the sky as if they had an urgent appointment somewhere in the next hemisphere. There were a bunch of people sitting at the tables, but they were not feeling the winds or looking up at the clouds. Instead, their heads were bent down — rather like the factory girls in Lianyungang, but instead of assembling cold-forged bicycle components they were intent on just one thing: licking the butter and garlic off their fingers.

Up close the truck resembled one of those roach coaches you often see at industrial parks selling sandwiches and tacos to workers. This one was different. Garlic shrimp, ONLY. A small, sharp-tongued Japanese woman appeared and started shouting at us: "Twelve shrimp, twelve dolla; twelve shrimp twelve dolla. How many you want? You want two?" I avoided eye contact. I knew she was the kind of salesperson who could peer right through my ragged defenses and get me to order more shrimp than I could possibly eat. So I avoided her gaze and a little like Pierce Brosnan I said, "Twelve dollars! That's lot of money for a dozen shrimp." "You get rice, fresh corn, salad and pineapple," she responded.

As Sue and I peeled away the thin shells from the hot buttery shrimp, I mumbled something like, "Aren't you glad I asked the concierge about the beer?" He had told us they did not have beer at the truck, but you could bring your own, which we did: a big cold can of Australian Foster's. We bit into the fluffy white flesh, infused with butter and garlic. We savored the first succulent taste. Our eyes met like in a movie, and all the world's most difficult questions: like how math works, when to refinance and who to blame for things; all the big questions of life were suddenly irrelevant. Our heads dropped. We sucked up the butter and garlic and shrimp; we sipped cold Foster's and licked our fingers in silence.

I feel Hillary's defeat was representative of the way events over the last two years had been jolting us out of our routine expectations. It had been happening all over the place, but we were so absorbed by the Ponzi schemes that make up our daily lives that we didn't pick up on the auspicious indicators of collapse. Remember when Djokovic, the arrogant Serb, beat Federer, the soft-spoken, stylish champion from Switzerland? That was a sign. And remember when the glossy New England Patriots were overrun by a more muscular and well armed New York Giants front line. That was a sign. And then Hillary Clinton's coronation, totally stolen by a skinny black guy whose dad herded goats in Kenya. Like the lines in your hands and patterns of grounds left at the bottom of your demitasse cup of Turkish coffee, these were signs that we just missed. And today, the collapse of the Ponzi scheme that the President of the United States, the Fed Chairman and the Secretary of the Treasury used to refer to as "the economy." We have to ask ourselves: were we dreaming then or are we dreaming now? But I must say it is consoling to see a man like Ben Bernanke as bewildered about his reality as I am about mine, and to watch as the dishonest, creaky U.S. establishment gets shouldered aside by what parents and self-righteous high school principals used to refer to as: consequences; giving way to a brave new world that is just beginning to come into view for my Lara, Taylor and Amanda. If I weren't so focused on the hummus, I'd have chills just thinking about it.

But wait!

It's two o'clock a.m. Lara's Jet Blue flight lands in Long Beach in about an hour and we have to go pick her up.

Sue always likes to get to the airport an hour or so early so we can wait in the cold and watch the long train of passengers walk through the terminal doors, one after another, until:

WAIT! There she IS! It's Lara!

Oh yes, she's finally home for Christmas, and after all she's been through in the last few arctic days, she's still aglow in her understated, stylish way. She's a tired world-weary young woman who has once again subdued the beast of winter and arrived home safely at three o'clock in the morning, into the arms of Mommy and Daddy. We hug like in a movie, cry like in a movie, tears running down Sue's cheeks and onto the small piece of Amanda's fudge we brought. "Oh, Merry Christmas, honey. Merry Christmas!"

My hope of course is that after reading the Christmas Letter and pondering the important issues it has raised about pita chips, cobblestones and the trade-off between kidneys and college tuition, that you will be better able to determine for yourselves what is genuine in your world and what is essentially a . . . you know: Ponzi scheme. By combining two eventful years into one letter, we have not only helped wean you off sports highlights, but have also been able to demonstrate a really big lesson: no two years are ever exactly the same, unless you work in China.

2007 began with pajamas and plum tomatoes in a cartoon-colored massage parlor in the middle of Beijing. 2008 began with a return to the hour "of splendour in the grass, of glory in the flower". But that was all about "us," and as I said earlier, a Christmas Letter should not become too absorbed with one's self and family, but should examine the broader sociological trends that have occurred in the world. One should inquire: what was the core difference between those two eventful journeys around the sun?

I tend to reduce the difference to one thing: a stark shift in enemies. In '07 we faced the clear and imminent danger of the very pious, the very poor and Hugo Chavez. Today you hardly hear anything about those guys, and instead our nation has been brought down in a devastating attack by . . . well . . . you know . . . like, by . . . ourselves. I mean who are the "Housing Market," the SEC, the FED, the Auto Industry and the Banks, if not us. So, it's pretty clear this year, this Christmas, that our biggest enemy turns out to be America, itself. And as you can imagine, that is a total bummer, because unlike those "foreign" enemies, there's no way we can do like a Bush Doctrine, I mean a preemptive strike against ourselves. That would be ridiculous. I of course realize, in all this confusion, you are probably looking to me for an answer, when you should be looking to the new president, Barak Obama.

Well, Okay. Obama's too new to know any answers. So, Merry Christmas: The answer lies in the concept of "enemy" itself, whether Hugo Chavez or the Cherokee Nation. I think Jesus tried – and failed — to expose the fallacy of "enemy," but that doesn't mean Jesus was wrong. It just means he needs to come back and try again. 'Til then, I'm sure Jessie was right-on when, while riding his bike around Lake Geneva and over the new Large Hadron Collider, he said to us,

"Life's too short to be small.
Be angels all, one unto another."

And have a Merry Christmas,
With our love,

Mark, Sue, Lara and Penny

2008
Important Events

- **XXIX Summer Olympics in Beijing, China.**
  Mark says, "I was there! Look! I pee'd right there!"

- **Sue learns to text.**
  First one is about scandal on Wisteria Lane.

- **JZ and Beyoncé marry.**
  Lara says it's a lot more important than Charles and Camilla.

- **Large Hadron Collider (LHC) is officially inaugurated at Geneva.**
  Daddy throws party for Higgs boson.

- **Lehman Brothers files Bankruptcy. Economy Collapses.**
  Republicans blame Hillary.

- **Barack Obama elected 44th President of the United States.**
  President Bush hands over keys and says, "Good luck, heh-heh!"

Lara makes it home for Christmas.

Whew!

Afterword

Yes. Lara made it "home for Christmas." And, just like the song, it was wonderful. She and Mommy decorated the two trees while I spent my free time complaining. Then we had the cabbage rolls, which were the best ever. I finally got to dip my Inca Chips into the hummus, too, which proved to be yet another Christmas miracle, because after my first gluttonous dip, the three of us believe we saw an image of Jesus appear on the serene bean surface. Wow. Talk about a good omen! The apparition didn't last long though, because we loved Mommy's hummus so much, we couldn't stop dipping into it and . . . well, just like last time, Jesus disappeared.

But he'll be back. And 'til then we all need to get to work. As you know, the New Millennium has had kind of a rocky start, what with the biggest economic collapse since the Great Depression and all. Then there's climate change. And how to work our iPhones. And what to do with Hillary. Clearly, the challenges are huge, but I know you're up to it. After all, if you have the staying power to finish this book, then you have what it takes to change the world. That's what we're going to do. Lara's taking the Northern Hemisphere. Sue's taking the South, plus all her inmates in the O.C. Jails. And I'm taking the rest. The good news is we have 998 years until the next New Millennium begins. So, plenty of time.

Just one note of caution. While you're engaged in the frenzied struggle to find gluten-free food, shelter with exactly the right square footage and a view, meet some celebrities and cough up tuition for your kids, just be sure you take some time to "live." Yes: "live." And pay attention to it. And whatever happens, put it all in your Christmas Letter.

Ocho Bonita

Acknowledgements

Like all books with a miniscule historical scope and dubious facts, *The Christmas Letters II, Laughing all the Way* would not have been possible without inspiration and help from a lot of other people. In spite of their objections to having their names made public, we feel an obligation to mention them here.

First and foremost, and for obvious reasons, I want to thank Mary and Joseph. It could not have been an easy trip. And without them, we'd be stuck writing the Hanukkah Letters, and let's face it: no one really knows how to spell Hanika.

Second of course, I need to give credit to Sir Isaac Newton for discovering gravity in 1687. Without this discovery the earth would not orbit the sun and winter would not exist. Just think what kind of Christmas that would be, right?

When you consider how important it has been to this book, not to mention to our daughter's development as a fully endowed citizen with all the rights and privileges thereof, it would be unconscionable not to acknowledge the California Department of Motor Vehicles. Thanks DMV, we couldn't have done it without you.

I am indebted to the Harriot & Harvey Trust for a Research Fellowship which enabled me to study in Paris where I discovered Christmas is actually conducted in French; to the School of Social Science and Yuletide Expository Writing at the Institute of Advanced Studies in Princeton where I studied the history of "Acknowledgements," and for a year's Fellowship from Charlotte and Abdul Aziz who were my neighbors and completely unaware of the Fellowship; they reported it as a burglary.

And Johnson's & Johnson's Baby Shampoo? My gosh. Who invented this stuff, anyway: soap that doesn't burn your eyes! I don't know which Johnson figured that out, but I certainly want to give credit where credit is due.

In our previous book we made sure to mention the originators of the Christmas Letter, early paleolithic men and women. And it's important to acknowledge them here, too. Even a cursory examination of the famous cave paintings from the time, reveals a bunch of parents in the process of bragging about their kids and sharing family vacations, which they called "hunting and gathering." Today, we write our letters on their shoulders, which is really awkward.

Still indebted to the Egyptians, too, especially for the letter "M," without which this book would not have been possible.

And Gutenberg? Yes! Thank you, Johannes. Movable type did for the Bible and long form Christmas Letter what the Internet did for zealotry and porn.

Needless to say, we owe a debt of gratitude that can never really be paid – unless we sell a lot of books – to Gertrude, Alice and Roman, our tireless fact checkers. They spent like fifteen minutes tracking down all the historical references and both of the facts contained in this book, and did all this without tires. Thanks guys!

Herman Melville is a writer I was particularly inspired by during my work on both the first Christmas Letters and Christmas Letters "Deux." Not too many people know that *Moby Dick* began as a Christmas Letter to Melville's second family, which he started – without telling his first family – on the island of Typee. It gets complicated, but the brilliant invention of the White Whale as a symbol for Santa Claus was forever with me in my own work. Thanks Herman, and your secret is safe with me.

A much belated thank you – and congratulations – to

Dr. Claude Beck for inventing the Cardiac Defibrillator. It saved my life more than once during the writing of this book.

And before I forget, I must also mention the actor, Edmund O'Brian.

An inordinate amount of credit must go to the aging process itself, for transforming the writer – in this case me – from a young, vibrant and some say reasonably handsome man into a guy people keep mistaking for Freddie Kruger. It wasn't until this process removed from my life all the other reasons for living, not to mention all the cartilage from my knees, that I realized writing Christmas Letters was the thing to do.

And of all the people I have to thank, no one deserves more gratitude than Omar, my go-to-guy at BevMo. During the entire process of researching – which was really mostly remembering stuff – writing and editing the manuscript, Omar was always there with recommendations for another cool craft beer from Montana. Omar taught me everything I know about hydration and the creative process, and for that I have given him my American Express account number, and the expiration date.

And finally, I would be remiss without mentioning the great Sam Peckinpah!

Lara pretends to laugh at Senator Diane Feinstein's jokes

About the Author

Before winning the Nobel Prize for the second time, Mark Mendizza was a . . . wait! He didn't win the Nobel Prize. Forget that. . .

He was a commercial writer. Clients said it was the funniest stuff they'd ever read, even when it was about serious subjects like how to change a bicycle spoke. He spent the 70's recovering from the 60's. And the 80's he lived as an expatriate in the Middle East, where he had the whole region laughing about his recipe for peppermint kabob. Then he got serious. He started a marketing company; got married to Sue; and spent the 90's in love, raising Lara. When Wordsworth said, "The child is the father of the man," he had Mark in mind. His latest book is about the experience and deep meaning of the ordinary family. It's fun. It's touching. It's ridiculous. Hey, It's family.

Lara, Bill & Kelly

"You know, you're Dad's a real spaz."

"Tell me about it."

"For everything that lives is Holy .

— William Blake